NOTES ON
'ESSENTIALS OF FAITH ALONE'

A Translation of Shinran's Yuishinshō-mon'i

NOTES ON
ESSENTIALS OF FAITH ALONE

A Translation of Shinran's Yuishinshō-mon'i

NOTES ON 'ESSENTIALS OF FAITH ALONE'

A Translation of
Shinran's Yuishinshō-mon'i

General Editor
Yoshifumi Ueda

SHIN BUDDHISM TRANSLATION SERIES
HONGWANJI INTERNATIONAL CENTER
Kyoto

Co-translators

Dennis Hirota, Head Translator
Michio Tokunaga, Kyoto Women's University
Taitetsu Unno, Smith College
Ryushin Uryuzu, Kyoto Women's University
Fumimaro Watanabe, Kinki University

Assistant

Takao Nishioka

Notes on 'Essentials of Faith Alone', copyright © 1979
by the Hongwanji International Center, Higashi-nakasuji,
Rokujo sagaru, Shimogyo-ku, Kyoto 600.
All rights reserved.

First edition

ISBN 4−938490−02−1
ISBN 0−859581−37E

Printed in Japan

PREFACE

His Eminence Koshin Ohtani assumed the responsibilities of transmitting the teaching of Shinran Shonin upon acceding to the seat of Monshu of Jodo Shinshu Hongwanji-ha on April 1, 1977, on the abdication by the Monshu Emeritus. Monshu Koshin Ohtani will formally announce to the Buddha and the Founding Shonin his accession and affirm his determination to propagate the teaching of Jodo Shinshu at the Accession Commemorative Celebrations in 1980.

In order that the Accession Commemorative Celebrations may become an occasion for one of the meaningful steps in the long-range program of our Hongwanji, many plans were inaugurated in 1979. In the area of international propagation a 12 year commemorative program, divided into 3 periods, for the translation and publication in English of the basic Canons of Jodo Shinshu was activated.

I am very happy to be able to present to the public, even before the start of the Accession Commemorative Celebrations, this book, NOTES ON 'ESSENTIALS OF FAITH ALONE', as the first result from the commemorative program. And I take this opportunity to express my deepest appreciation to everyone concerned for their efforts in its translation and publication.

I sincerely hope that Shinran Shonin's persuasion may be understood truly and deeply by all who shall read this book.

> BISHOP DAIJUN TOYOHARA
> Director General
> JODO SHINSHU HONGWANJI-HA

CONTENTS

CONTENTS

INTRODUCTION

To understand the teaching of Shinran (1173–1262), the founder of Jōdo Shinshū, or Shin Buddhism, we must listen carefully and precisely to what he has to say in his writings. Among his works, three form a unique genre of extended notes on well-known passages from Pure Land sources. Written by Shinran when he was between seventy-eight and eighty-six, at the end of his highly productive life, they express his most mature thought.

The three works are *Notes on 'Essentials of Faith Alone'* (1250), *Notes on 'Once-calling and Many-calling'* (1257), and *Notes on the Inscriptions on Sacred Scrolls* (shorter version, 1255; longer version, 1258). The first two are Shinran's exegeses of passages in Chinese quoted in tracts by fellow disciples of Hōnen, *The Essentials of Faith Alone* by Seikaku (1166–1235) and *The Clarification of Once-calling and Many-calling* by Ryūkan (1148–1227). The third work is a commentary on the scriptural texts included on hanging scrolls inscribed with the holy Name, namu-amida-butsu or its equivalents, or on portraits of venerable teachers in the Pure Land tradition.

Although the last decade of Shinran's life was characterized by inner and outer turmoil, as evident in the extant letters to his followers, these three works, written during this period, give testimony to his resilient spirituality and creative mind. In them we see Shinran not only inheriting the basic ideas of Hōnen and manifesting ever more clearly the centrality of Other Power, but also articulating his own unique and revolutionary views on Pure Land practice and thought.

Although Shinran strongly encouraged his own followers to study *The Essentials of Faith Alone* as a faithful presentation of Hōnen's teaching, he also felt the need to explain in simpler language, and at the same time with far greater insight, some of the key concepts contained in the work. When we compare Seikaku's original and Shinran's *Notes*, we clearly discern aspects of continuity with the Pure Land tradition as well as points of radical change. With Shinran, the Pure Land teaching underwent a major transformation, and Mahayana Buddhism attained yet another evolutionary peak.

Nirvana as Fundamental

The goal of Buddhism is nirvana, which is attained through the extinction of blind passion and the seeing of things, including the self, as they truly are. The ultimate end of the Pure Land path is also nirvana, its uniqueness lying in the boundless compassion of Amida, transcending all conceivable forms of love or mercy, which "brings all sentient beings into the supreme nirvana" (page 30). Shinran's own understanding of what constitutes nirvana and how it is an integral part of the human reality is given in his comments on the quotation, "The land of bliss is the realm of nirvana, the uncreated." Although Seikaku offers no comment on this line, Shinran explains it in detail, stating that "the realm of nirvana refers to the place where one overturns the delusion of ignorance and realizes the supreme enlightenment" (page 42). Nirvana, he says, has many synonyms, some of which have religious overtones—extinction of passions, peaceful happiness, eternal bliss, oneness, and Buddha-nature—and others ontological connotations, such as the uncreated, true reality, dharmakaya, dharma-nature, and suchness. He then concludes, "Buddha-nature is none other than Tathagata. This Tathagata pervades the countless worlds; it fills the hearts and minds of the ocean of all beings. Thus, plants, trees, and land all attain Buddhahood" (page 42). This Tathagata is known as the dharmakaya-as-suchness, which will be discussed later.

Here we see a distinctive characteristic of Mahayana thought that differentiates it from Western religions, with their clear dichotomy between creator and created, and between man and nature, and also from modern scientific thought, which draws a sharp division between animate and inanimate existence. The Buddhist way of thinking, as just exemplified in Shinran's words, cannot be categorized as pantheism, as is frequently done, since there is no "being" that stands against the world, the Tathagata being formless and nameless. The Tathagata is simply a fact fundamental not only to the human condition but to all existence—including trees, plants, rocks, and all forms of life—seen through the eyes of satori or enlightenment.

Shinran says that it is this heart and mind, pervaded by the formless and nameless Tathagata, that entrusts itself to the Primal Vow of the dharmakaya-as-compassion. The latter is none other than Amida Buddha, appearing in history as the Name, namu-amida-butsu, and manifesting its unseen but powerful working as Unhindered Light. Instead of calling this working "Amida" here, Shinran uses the term "dharmakaya-as-compassion" to clarify its unitary relationship to the dharmakaya-as-suchness.

Twofold Dharmakaya

In general, the term "dharmakaya" is used in Mahayana Buddhism only to refer to the formless and nameless Tathagata, without distinguishing between dharmakaya-as-suchness and dharmakaya-as-compassion. Following the preceding discussion, however, Shinran states, "There are two kinds of dharmakaya in regard to the Buddha." These two kinds of dharmakaya are distinct and separate, for dharmakaya-as-suchness has no form or characteristics, and is beyond conceptualization, while dharmakaya-as-compassion possesses form and characteristics, appearing as Amida Buddha, and hence lies within human comprehension. But at the same time they are inseparable, for dharmakaya-as-compassion also has a dimension which is without form or characteristics. The relationship between these two kinds of dharmakaya was first enunciated by T'an-luan, in a passage quoted by Shinran in his *Kyōgyōshinshō*:

> Among Buddhas and bodhisattvas there are two aspects of dharmakaya: dharmakaya-as-suchness and dharmakaya-as-compassion. Dharmakaya-as-compassion arises out of dharmakaya-as-suchness, and dharmakaya-as-suchness emerges into [human consciousness through] dharmakaya-as-compassion. These two aspects of dharmakaya differ but are not separate; they are one but not identical.

This dynamic relationship between the two is expressed variously by Shinran. In his *Notes*, for example, he writes, "From this oneness (dharmakaya-as-suchness), was manifested form, called dharmakaya-as-compassion. Taking this form, the Buddha proclaimed his name as Bhikṣu Dharmākara and established the forty-eight Vows" (page 43). A similar passage is found in his *Notes on 'Once-calling and Many-calling'*: "Compassionate means refers to manifesting form, taking a Name, and making itself known to sentient beings." Shinran elaborates this point in a letter:

> The supreme Buddha (dharmakaya-as-suchness) is formless, and because of being formless is called *jinen* .... In order to make us realize that the true Buddha is formless, it is expressly called Amida Buddha, so I have been taught. Amida Buddha is the medium through which we are made to realize jinen. (*Letters of Shinran*, Letter 5)

In summary, then, the ultimate formless and nameless dharmakaya-as-suchness (nirvana) manifests itself in the world as Amida Buddha, dharmakaya-as-compassion, emerging in this samsaric ocean to make itself comprehensible to men. Comprehension here does not mean mere intellectual assent; it involves the transformation of the whole person encountering dharmakaya-as-compassion.

Foolish Being

Since most forms of Mahayana Buddhism speak only of the formless and nameless dharmakaya, why did Shinran invoke Amida, the dharmakaya-as-compassion? The reason lies in the totally different structure of religious experience and realization. Zen, for example, aims relentlessly for the realization of non-self, stripping away the individualizing characteristics and marks of all objects, thus transcending the subject-object dichotomy, or objectifying thought, to bring to realization the formless and nameless reality. Whatever reflection or religiosity there is in Zen thought is meant to deepen the experience of transcendence in dharmakaya-as-suchness.

Shin Buddhism, however, speaks from the standpoint of one bound to the karmic self, whether it be called finite existence philosophically or foolish being religiously. To such a person—possessing a self, incapable of religious austerities, and devoid even of potential wisdom—Amida Buddha, with name and form, directs his compassion in the Primal Vow. In other words, dharmakaya-as-compassion is moved to encounter this foolish being living in the subject-object dichotomous world. Here it is essential that we understand what it is to be "foolish." Foolish is not a relative term contrasted to intelligent or wise; it applies to one who, turning to the religious quest to go beyond samsaric existence, discovers the utter impossibility of such a task. In the words of Shinran, "The Primal Vow was established out of deep compassion for us who cannot become freed from the bondage of birth-and-death through any religious practice, due to the massiveness of blind passion" (*Tannishō* III). Such a person, born of deep religious awakening, is also called a being of karmic evil, because the roots of his evil are so profound that it is beyond comprehension (hence, "karmic"), creating countless seen and unseen sufferings for himself and others (hence, "evil").

Because of the powerful bondage that characterizes the foolish being, traditional paths to enlightenment are closed and the only avenue open to him is to "hear" the origin and purpose of the Primal Vow: the compassionate design of Amida for the being incapable of any religious practice that will lead to the supreme enlightenment. When this design of Amida to carry all beings to enlightenment reaches the depth of his heart, deeper than intellectual understanding, he is made to awaken to the great compassion of Amida. This is none other than to be made to entrust himself to the act of great compassion and realize the full dimension of what is heard.

This awakening of the foolish being, not as decision or commitment but as the manifestation of Amida's working, is called *shinjin*. Shinjin has two aspects: first it is the act of

7

entrusting oneself to Amida by virtue of the Primal Vow; and second, it is the true and real mind and heart of Amida Buddha, in contrast to the false and vain heart and mind of man. The second aspect is the basis for the first. Since this entrusting is all due to true compassion, no room is found for any kind of willful calculation or self-assertion. In the realization of one's foolishness and karmic bondage and of the overwhelming magnitude of Other Power, all self-power has been eradicated.

Shinjin: The Experience of Being Transformed

Shinjin has been frequently translated as "faith," but this may be misleading. If it were merely a matter of believing in scripture, or placing faith in the Buddha, or anticipating a future life in the Pure Land, faith may be acceptable, but shinjin is not a matter of blind trust, vulnerable to uncertainties and anxieties. Rather, shinjin is born from an awakening to the fathomless evil of oneself made possible through the working of Amida; at its core is a kind of wisdom that comes with the realization of things, including the self, as they truly are. Shinjin, however, is more than wisdom; there is a radical transformation in which evil (the good and evil of the foolish being) becomes good (the good of the Buddha), occurring at the depths of one's being. This transformation takes place the moment shinjin is realized and continues to take place, for the mind of blind passion which arises from deep in the unconscious cannot be easily transformed into great compassion. Shinran expresses the concept of transformation (*ten*) as follows:

"To be made to become so" means that without the practicer's calculating in any way whatsoever, all his past, present, and future evil karma is transformed into the highest good. To be transformed means that evil karma, without being nullified or eradicated, is made into the highest good, just as all waters, upon entering the great ocean, immediately become ocean water (page 32).

This is expressed in a more concrete metaphor when he states: "When we entrust ourselves to the Tathagata's Primal Vow, we, who are like bits of tile and pebbles, are turned into gold" (pages 40–41). Another favorite metaphorical expression used by Shinran to express this transformation is found in *The Hymns on the Patriarchs*:

> Having gained shinjin majestic and profound
> By virtue of Unhindered Light,
> The ice of blind passion melts without fail
> To instantly become the water of enlightenment.

It now becomes evident that the Mahayana ideal of the universality of Buddha-nature receives a new, existential formulation in Shin Buddhism. The foolish being, lacking true and real mind, is devoid of Buddha-nature as far as his own reality is concerned, but in the miraculous transformation wrought by the Primal Vow, he is brought to an awareness of shinjin, which is the working of Tathagata, and where the working is actualized, Buddha-nature becomes a reality, not a mere ideal.

> The person who rejoices in shinjin
> Is equal to Tathagatas, so it is taught.

> Great shinjin is Buddha-nature,
> Buddha-nature is Tathagata itself.

Attaining the Stage of Non-retrogression

In the career of the Mahayana bodhisattva, from the initial aspiration for enlightenment to the final, ultimate realization, the crucial stage is that of non-retrogression. It is not enough merely to perform altruistic deeds or advance through the various stages of achievements; the bodhisattva must attain (*prativedha*) to suchness and come into contact (*spṛśate*) with reality as dharmakaya. At this point the bodhisattva's mind, finite and karma-created, becomes one with the infinite, uncreated Tathagata. For the first time in the course of his religious practice he goes beyond temporal samsaric existence and realizes transcendence. Here the bodhisattva experiences non-retrogression, for there is no longer any fear of backsliding or regressing to lower stages, the realm of samsara. Unifying both time and timelessness, the finite and infinite, samsara and nirvana, he touches Tathagata and experiences enlightenment. But because of the vestiges of blind passion, hidden beneath the surface of consciousness and obstructing it, enlightenment has yet to become fully manifest. He must undergo further religious training until the last remnants of his karmic life become exhausted to realize Tathagatahood fully.

In Zen Buddhism, non-retrogression is attained in this life through discipline and practice that lead to the direct realization of dharmakaya-as-suchness. In traditional Pure

Land practice this stage was to be attained in the land of the Buddhas after death. Shinran, however, asserted that when a person realizes shinjin, he dwells in the stage of non-retrogression, which he also called the stage of the truly settled or the equal of enlightenment. All this is accomplished here and now in the immediate moment of shinjin, "without any passage of time and without any passage of days," not in some distant, unknown future. For Shinran, then, shinjin corresponds to the experience of the bodhisattva who has seen suchness and touched the reality of dharmakaya. Because of the working of Amida's compassion, the attainment of highest Buddhahood is only a matter of time for the person who entrusts himself to the Primal Vow.

To appreciate fully Shinran's concept of shinjin, we must briefly trace the evolution of the idea of *ōjō*, or "going to be born" in the Pure Land, and his radical reinterpretation.

Birth in the Pure Land

The traditional view at the heart of the Pure Land transmission was the belief that a person would be born in the Pure Land after death, receive the aid of the Buddha, attain non-retrogression, and ultimately realize highest enlightenment. It would be the ideal realm for pursuing the path to enlightenment, and it became the goal of the religious life for many monks and lay people alike down through the centuries. Shinran, however, redefined the concept of birth in the Pure Land, based upon his own deep penetration into the compassion of the Buddha, and expanded it to cover two fundamental dimensions. First, "birth in the Pure Land" is to attain the stage of non-retrogression; second, it is synonymous with the attainment of supreme enlightenment or Buddhahood at the very moment of death. Both ideas represented a revolutionary break with the accepted view of what it meant to be born in the Pure Land. Let us briefly summarize the earlier views regarding this central notion in Pure Land Buddhism.

Among the seven Pure Land patriarchs enumerated by Shinran, Nāgārjuna (third century A.D.) taught that non-retrogression could be attained in this life by either the path of difficult practice or that of easy practice. But subsequent patriarchs all encouraged people to aspire for birth in the Pure Land after death to attain the stage of non-retrogression by receiving the aid of the Buddha. Especially in periods of acute spiritual crises, filled with the five defilements and historically distant from Śākyamuni Buddha, the desire to be born in the Pure Land became increasingly popular and powerful. Hōnen, more than any other patriarch, clarified the power of the Primal Vow to carry the faithful to the Pure Land where he could attain non-retrogression and realize enlightenment. Stressing exclusive practice of recitative nembutsu, as did Shan-tao and others, he made Buddhism relevant to the times and the needs of ordinary people.

Throughout his long life, Shinran showed unswerving devotion to his master's teaching, and yet, having delved into Hōnen's teaching to its very source, the Primal Vow of Amida, he went beyond traditional views and affirmed the experience of non-retrogressive stage in this life. In the words of Shinran:

Then they attain birth means that when a person realizes shinjin, he is born immediately. "To be born immediately" is to dwell in the stage of non-retrogression. To dwell in the stage of non-retrogression is to become established in the stage of the truly settled. This is also called the attainment of the equal of perfect enlightenment. Such is the meaning of **then they attain birth. Then** means "immediately"; "immediately" means without any passage of time and without any passage of days (pages 34–5).

Shinjin, thus, is not mere faith or entrusting; it is a fundamental religious experience in the here and now of Amida's compassion, the realm of infinite wisdom transcending samsaric life. The Pure Land path as seen by Shinran not only leads to non-retrogression in this life, but to the realization of supreme enlightenment at the very moment of death. This view was also unheard of in the history of Buddhism.

The Salvation of All Beings

The traditional view was that a long period of spiritual discipleship in the Pure Land was necessary before one could attain supreme enlightenment, but Shinran taught that the person of shinjin attains Buddhahood at the moment of death, having become free from karmic limitations. Moreover, Shinran reinterprets the term *rai*, which traditionally referred to the Buddha's "coming" to welcome the faithful at the moment of death (pages 33–4). The true meaning of "Amida's coming" is that the Tathagata makes beings "come" to the

Pure Land, rejecting the defiled land and aspiring for the true, fulfilled land. Further, *rai* means "to return," which is to attain supreme enlightenment without fail, having entered the ocean of the Vow. This is returning to the "city of dharma-nature," where a person also experiences true reality or suchness, the uncreated or dharmakaya, emancipation, eternal bliss of dharma-nature, and supreme enlightenment. But this return again focuses on this samsaric world:

> When a person attains this enlightenment, with great love and great compassion immediately reaching their fullness in him, he returns to the ocean of birth-and-death to save all sentient beings; this is known as attaining the virtue of Bodhisattva Samantabhadra. To attain this benefit is **come**; that is, "to return to the city of dharma-nature" (pages 33–4).

According to Shinran, the goal of the Pure Land tradition is to return into the samsaric world to work for the salvation of all beings. This is precisely the bodhisattva ideal of Mahayana Buddhism, contained in the concept of the nirvana of no-abode (*apratiṣṭhita-nirvāṇa*) where one gains non-dichotomous wisdom (*nirvikalpa-jñāna*, which is synonymous with *prajñā-pāramitā*), so that all barriers between samsara and nirvana are lifted. The bodhisattva experiences these contradictory opposites as a unitary reality, which is the ground for the manifestation of wisdom and compassion—wisdom delivering man from samsara for entry into nirvana and compassion freeing him from nirvana for involvement in samsara. The same relationship holds between our karma-bound world and the Pure Land of freedom for the person of shinjin, who has plumbed the depths of Buddha's wisdom and compassion by virtue of the Primal Vow.

Essentially, the bodhisattva serves all beings without discrimination and the benefits of his deed are shared equally by all, including himself, due to the all-inclusive nature of non-dichotomous wisdom. Shinran expresses this same understanding, having been grasped by Amida and having attained the non-retrogressive stage of the bodhisattva. Thus, he could say that "All beings are fathers and mothers, brothers and sisters, in the timeless process of birth-and-death" (*Tannishō* v).

Ultimately, the shinjin of Other Power manifests the central concern of Mahayana Buddhism, as summarized by Shinran in his *Notes*:

> Bodhisattva Vasubandhu declares that this true and real shinjin is none other than the aspiration to become a Buddha. This is the great thought of enlightenment of the Pure Land. This aspiration for Buddhahood is none other than the wish to save all beings. The wish to save all beings is the wish to carry all beings across the great ocean of birth-and-death. This shinjin is the aspiration to bring all beings to the attainment of supreme nirvana; it is the heart of great love and great compassion. This shinjin is Buddha-nature and Buddha-nature is Tathagata (pages 45–6).

Thus, the aspiration to be born in the Pure Land is not some kind of world-weary escapism nor religious sentimentality; rather, it becomes the most powerful expression of bodhisattvic compassion, the most enduring form of universal care and concern. In spite of its depth and scope, however, shinjin is still an awareness in the foolish being, who himself can never cherish the wish to save all beings in the true sense, because of his karmic limitations. Shinjin definitely contains the wisdom of Buddha, but it is clouded by ignorance. Here we have the paradox that some measure of compassion comes through the awareness of the foolish being who admits his total incapacity for good, or in the words of Shinran:

> The compassion in the path of Pure Land is to first of all become a Buddha, saying the nembutsu, and with the heart of great compassion and love save all beings as we desire . . . . Only the saying of nembutsu is the complete and thoroughgoing compassion that is true, real, and sincere (*Tannishō* IV).

Shinran's Originality

Notes on 'Essentials of Faith Alone' consists of quotations in Chinese from the Pure Land Buddhist canon together with detailed explanations of their meaning and significance in Japanese. It is often pointed out, however, that Shinran's interpretations do not always correspond with the original meaning of the passages. This is usually explained as indicating that Shinran had arrived at his own personal understanding, which differed from that of the accepted Pure Land teaching. It is not enough, however, simply to recognize that these differences exist, for not only did Shinran hold the tradition in profound reverence, but he also had extensive training in Chinese, and these two facts more than ensure that he knew well the literal meaning of the passages. We must go on to ask, then, what it was that compelled him to give bold, new interpretations that departed from, and at times even contradicted, the traditional understandings, interpretations that at points might be said to be forced, unnatural, and unjustified by the Chinese text.

One of the most fundamental and crucial instances of such a difference can be found in Shinran's interpretation of the passage from the *Larger Sutra* expressing the fulfillment of the Eighteenth Vow:

> When sentient beings hear the Name, have joy in a trusting mind even but one moment, with sincerity turn over merits [toward birth], and aspire to be born in that land, then they attain birth and dwell in the stage of non-retrogression.

In the sutra this passage means that one is born in the Pure Land after life in this world has ended, and there comes to dwell in the stage of non-retrogression. As we have seen, however, according to Shinran's interpretation, "**Then they attain birth** means that when a person realizes shinjin, he is born immediately. To be born immediately is to dwell in the stage of non-retrogression." This teaching that one could attain birth and dwell in the stage of non-retrogression in this life had never before appeared in the history of Pure Land Buddhism, in India, China, or Japan, and it clearly contradicts the traditional explanations.

Some historians of Buddhist thought have been highly critical of Shinran, stating that he makes light of the basic texts by quoting from them arbitrarily without the least regard for the context and original meaning. However, since there was no outside pressure which forced Shinran to make such interpretations, what made it necessary for him to do so was undoubtedly something spiritual that came from within himself. This fact requires careful consideration, for it involves the special quality of religious awakening in Buddhism.

What is called satori or enlightenment is said to be a wholly personal and direct kind of knowing. It is the realization of suchness (*tathatā*) occurring within one's total being and not dependent upon any kind of outside authority or external power, even if it be an enlightened master or a Buddha. This was the basic experience of Śākyamuni, of Nāgārjuna, Asaṅga, and Vasubandhu, and of great Zen masters. The *Laṅkāvatāra Sūtra* calls it "the realization of wisdom of self-knowledge" (*svapratyātmāryajñāna*). What Shinran calls shinjin also falls within this purview: he came to know with certainty, having deeply touched the heart of Amida that is one with formless and nameless dharmakaya, that shinjin constitutes the attainment of non-retrogression. It is not just a subjective feeling. In fact, all traces of subjectivity—intellectual or otherwise— have been swept away, and all kinds of self-centered notions have been purged in his fundamental realization as a foolish being. While Shinran speaks as a foolish being, he is now contained within the wisdom of Amida; therefore, what he says comes from that transcendental reality. In short, Shinran now reads the sutra, which contains the words of Śākyamuni, through the eyes of the wisdom of Amida, the dharmakaya-as-compassion, which is the source and inspiration of all sutras. The wisdom of Amida from which he speaks transcends the conventional words and logic by which Amida's Primal Vow is taught and goes to the very foundation of existence itself, and even beyond it to timeless and immeasurable life.

Emerging from the depth of Amida's wisdom, which is fundamental, Shinran articulated a fresh and original vision of what it means to be truly human. To understand the Buddha's teaching one cannot merely follow the words of the scriptures; one must go deep into the source from which they came. In Shinran this was accomplished in shinjin, where he became identified with Amida's wisdom.

In a most real sense, then, Shinran the radical reformer was true to the heart of the Pure Land tradition. No one can maintain a living tradition without delving deeply into its source, and no one can extend it into the future by making light of the inherited tradition. Shinran plunged into the source of the Pure Land teaching, more deeply than anyone before or since, and as a result it was only natural that his radical reinterpretations went beyond traditional Pure Land teachings, which were futuristic and otherworldly. He thus established the Pure Land teaching firmly in the fundamental position of Mahayana Buddhism, a position of deep penetration into timelessness in the present moment, based upon the experience of twofold dharmakaya.

Hōnen and Shinran

Hōnen (also known as Genkū) proclaimed the basis of an

independent Pure Land school in 1175, and Shinran joined his ranks in 1201, after descending from the Tendai monastery atop Mount Hiei. A major nembutsu persecution occurred in 1207, and Shinran was forever separated from his beloved teacher; both were exiled to remote provinces in opposite directions. But his complete devotion to Hōnen remained unchanged throughout his life, as evidenced in *The Hymns on the Patriarchs*, written in 1248 when Shinran was seventy-six:

> Even through aeons of samsaric wanderings
> > Never knew I the crucial moment of deliverance.
> Had it not been for my teacher Genkū
> > This life, too, would have passed in vain.

> By the power of Wisdom Light
> > Appeared my teacher Genkū
> And proclaiming the true essence of the Pure Land
> > teaching
> Made known the selected Primal Vow.

In *Tannishō* II this reverence for his master is expressed in almost unbelievable words: "I have nothing to regret, even if I have been deceived by my teacher Hōnen, and saying the nembutsu should fall into hell."

What Shinran learned from his teacher and held close to his heart throughout his lifetime was simply, "Just say the nembutsu and be saved by Amida" (*Tannishō* II). When contrasted to the traditional requirement to master the Three Learnings of precepts, meditation, and wisdom, the simplicity of this new teaching was deceptive. It was only natural that few could appreciate that which gave this practice its awesome weight and power—the Primal Vow of Amida, directing boundless compassion to all beings. In contrast to the religious practices precariously balanced on finite human powers, the nembutsu is upheld by the infinite power of Amida Buddha, firmly rooted in the dharmakaya-as-suchness.

Hōnen's advocacy of the single practice of recitative nembutsu as the only efficacious path to enlightenment in the Latter Ages (*mappō*) is based upon his principle of selection and rejection. The selection of nembutsu by the Primal Vow as the sole, viable practice meant automatically the rejection of all existing Buddhist disciplines as ineffectual and meaningless. This denunciation of traditional Buddhism, helped by the historical sense of doom that filled the people's minds, was made possible by Hōnen's deep insight into Amida's wisdom and did not rest on fallible human judgment. He showed that limited self-power could never lead to supreme enlightenment; only that power coming from supreme enlightenment itself could effectuate the enlightenment of all beings, including those excluded from entering the gates of traditional Buddhist practices.

Shinran carried on the essential teaching of Hōnen, but he was also sensitive to the elements of self-assertion lurking hidden behind the Other Power practice of nembutsu. He, therefore, devoted his efforts to clarifying the necessity of being carried on the power of the Primal Vow as the inner dynamics of recitative nembutsu. The complete entrusting of self to the Primal Vow meant simultaneously abandoning all need to rely on self-power. This is the reason for Shinran's stress on shinjin, "the true and real mind of Amida Buddha," which is the source of this entrusting. Through the working of Amida's wisdom and compassion, we are made to say the nembutsu, affirming the enduring power of Amida and acknowledging our limited human capacities. Thus the central question for the Shin Buddhist becomes, not "How can I attain satori?," but "How can I be carried by the power of the Primal Vow?"

Seikaku and Shinran

In comparing the thought of Seikaku and Shinran, we see again Shinran underscoring the power of the Primal Vow, which works in every sphere of life and leaves no room at all for the justification of self-power. Seikaku, the author of *The Essentials of Faith Alone*, was born in 1167 and was six years Shinran's senior. He was of aristocratic birth and remained a Tendai monk throughout his life, even though he joined Hōnen's Pure Land movement. Both are possible reasons for his escaping the nembutsu persecution of 1207, when his teacher Hōnen and several fellow disciples, including Shinran, were exiled to remote provinces.

Hōnen the teacher regarded Seikaku highly as a spokesman for the new movement, and Shinran not only recommended *The Essentials of Faith Alone* to others but made at least six copies in his own handwriting to distribute to his own followers. It is clear that Seikaku played an important role in the transmission of Hōnen's teaching to Shinran, but there are some basic differences between them. Let us now look at some of the more important differences.

Shinran writes in his *Notes on 'Essentials of Faith Alone'* as follows: "To be free of self-power, having entrusted oneself to the Other Power of the Primal Vow—this is **faith alone**" (page 29). Both Seikaku and Shinran emphasize the importance of entrusting to Other Power, but Shinran realized in a more thorough and penetrating way than either Hōnen or Seikaku that entrusting also meant becoming free of self-power and of doubt regarding the efficacy of the Vow. The freedom from self-power is especially crucial because it makes clear that shinjin is not dependent upon the state of mind, intellectual or emotional, of the practicer but solely upon the working of the Primal Vow. This is alluded to by Shinran in the opening comments of his *Notes*:

> **Alone** means "this one thing only," expressing a rejection of two things standing together. It also means "by itself" . . . . Nothing is placed equal with this shinjin of Other Power, for it is the working of the universal Primal Vow (page 29).

To become free of self-power means to become free of and not depend upon the false and untrue, which constitutes the nature of the thoughts, words, and actions of human beings, as well as the society that surrounds us. In this world that which is true and real is nonexistent; only the Buddha is true, real, and sincere. In the words of Shinran:

> In this foolish being filled with blind passion and in this impermanent world, a burning house, all things are empty and vain, and, therefore, untrue. Only the nembutsu is true, real and sincere (*Tannishō*, Epilogue).

In contrast to Seikaku who emphasizes the simplicity and efficacy of recitative nembutsu, Shinran places stress upon the working of the Primal Vow. When a person is carried by the power of the Primal Vow, he naturally and automatically is born in the Pure Land. This means that the daily life of the person of shinjin is permeated with Amida's compassion and that the Primal Vow brings to highest fulfillment every moment within it. Thus, shinjin here and now contains all those ideals that were once sought in the future: attaining the non-retrogressive stage, becoming truly settled, being equal to enlightenment, and settling one's birth in the Pure Land. Since Amida's activity to save all beings appears as shinjin in the hearts and minds of people, even the saying of the nembutsu is due to the working of the Primal Vow. Recitative nembutsu, thus, is not a means to some end but the end appearing in every moment of one's life. Shinran states:

> Since those people who are to be born in the true fulfilled land are without fail taken into the heart of the Buddha of unhindered light, they realize diamond-like shinjin. Thus, they "abundantly say the Name" (pages 39–40).

Another important topic traditionally is the mental attitude a person brings to the Pure Land path. The *Meditation Sutra* refers to three essential components—sincere mind, deep mind, and desire for birth by accumulating merit. Seikaku states that even if one of these is missing, the person will not attain birth in the Pure Land. Shinran, however, understands the three minds to be identical with the threefold shinjin in the *Larger Sutra*, and they are united in what he calls One-mind, based upon Vasubandhu's invocation, "With One-mind I worship the Buddha." Shinran states that this One-mind is none other than Other Power and concludes that where One-mind is missing, the person will not be born in the Pure Land. What was understood to be the essential mental attitudes of a person is now understood to be the manifestation of Other Power working in the heart and mind.

A related discussion concerns the interpretation of the passage that reads: "Do not express outwardly signs of wisdom, goodness, or diligence, while inwardly possessing that which is empty and transitory" (page 66). For Seikaku this meant that there should be no discrepancy between what a person is within and without, but for Shinran, who understood it within the realization of shinjin, such genuineness was totally impossible for a karma-bound being. Thus, he read the statement in an entirely different way:

We should not express outwardly signs of wisdom, goodness, or diligence, for inwardly we possess that which is empty and transitory (pages 48–9).

This is based on the realization of one's falseness and vanity, illuminated by true compassion, and contrasted to Other Power, which is true and real.

In conclusion, both Seikaku and Shinran advocated the central importance of recitative nembutsu and the power of the Primal Vow. Seikaku, however, appears to be speaking from the standpoint of the practicer, whereas Shinran always speaks from the position of one who is carried by the Primal Vow. Seikaku also stresses faith as an essential human act, merit, or practice, but Shinran emphasizes the working of the Primal Vow, which appears in man as shinjin. He sees no value whatsoever in man's saying of the nembutsu if it is merely a matter of utterance; Shinran's saying of the nembutsu must always includes shinjin.

A Note on the Translation

It may be useful here to set forth the principles which have guided the translation. Broadly speaking, two sorts of translation have seemed possible; to borrow the terms of Arthur Waley, they are the "literary" and the "philological." The former attempts to capture the literary qualities and the force of the original, while the latter strives to reproduce what is being said with detailed accuracy. *Notes on 'Essentials of Faith Alone'*, because it consists largely of close explications of words and phrases, cannot be said to possess great merit as a work of literature, and we have not attempted to impart to the text any literary qualities beyond its own succinctness and general clarity. Nevertheless, in practice we have constantly felt drawn in two directions, both by the demand for natural, lucid English and by the concern to transmit with fidelity what Shinran has written, often in language employing technical terms and structures of explanation that have no common counterpart in English. Our sole aim, however, has been to reproduce the work so that it might be useful in guiding the reader to an understanding of the core of Shinran's teaching, the religious transformation called shinjin, and therefore we have chosen, whenever we felt it necessary, to sacrifice naturalness or elegance of English in favor of a meticulous faithfulness to the original text. This, in any case, has been our governing principle.

We have also been concerned to translate special terms with consistency, so that contexts might begin to illuminate content in a dependable manner. The more important terms are included in the Glossary, where they are explained with special reference to their usage in the present work.

Notes on 'Essentials of Faith Alone' is not a commentary on Seikaku's *Essentials of Faith Alone* itself, but rather a series of explanations of passages in Chinese quoted by Seikaku, generally in the order of appearance in Seikaku's work. There is, therefore, no overall thematic development or formal structure unifying the *Notes*. Shinran's method, however, provides a clear view of his understanding of important passages from the Pure Land scriptures, and as discussed above, allows for a detailed comparison with the interpretations of the Pure Land tradition that went before him.

When translating the scriptural quotations in Shinran's *Notes*, we have taken into account Shinran's own explanations. Thus, in several instances—notably the quotations from Shan-tao concerning the three aspects or minds of faith (page 47) and the admonition against hypocrisy (pages 48–9)—the translation differs from that in Seikaku's *Essentials*, where the usage of the quotations closely follows traditional interpretation.

Bibliographic information on the texts we have followed can be found in a note on pages 112–4.

NOTES ON 'ESSENTIALS OF FAITH ALONE'

BY SHINRAN

In the title, *The Essentials of Faith Alone,* **alone** means "this one thing only," expressing a rejection of two things standing together. It also means "by itself."

Faith is the heart and mind without doubt; it is shinjin, which is true and real. It is the heart and mind free of that which is empty and transitory. Empty means "vain"; transitory means "provisional." Empty means "not real" and "not sincere"; transitory means "not true." To be free of self-power, having entrusted oneself to the Other Power of the Primal Vow—this is **faith alone**. **Essentials** indicates the selecting and gathering together of significant passages from the scriptures. Thus the title, *The Essentials of Faith Alone*.

Faith alone also means that nothing is placed equal with this shinjin of Other Power, for it is the working of the universal Primal Vow.

∽∾∾ ∽∾∾ ∽∾∾

The holy Name of the Tathagata is exceedingly distinct
   and clear;
Throughout the worlds in the ten quarters it prevails.
Only those who say the Name all attain birth;
Avalokiteśvara and Mahāsthāmaprāpta come of themselves
   to welcome them.[1]

The holy Name of the Tathagata is exceedingly distinct and clear

The Tathagata is the Tathagata of unhindered light. **The holy Name** is namu-amida-butsu. **Holy** means "sacred," "excellent." **Name** (*gō*) indicates the name of a Buddha after the attainment of Buddhahood; another term (*myō*) indicates his name before this attainment. The holy Name of the Tathagata surpasses measure, description, and conceptual understanding; it is the Name of the Vow embodying great love and great compassion, which brings all sentient beings into the supreme nirvana. The Name of this Buddha surpasses the names of all the other Tathagatas, for it is based on the Vow to save all beings.

Exceedingly distinct and clear: exceedingly here means "utterly," "unsurpassed." **Distinct** implies "to distinguish"; here it means to distinguish each sentient being. **Clear** means "evident." It is evident that Amida, distinguishing every

---

1. Quoted in *The Essentials of Faith Alone*, p. 59. Originally from *Hymns of the Nembutsu Liturgy in Fivefold Harmony* by Fa-chao (see "List of Names and Titles," p. 110).

sentient being in the ten quarters, guides each to salvation; thus his compassionate concern for us is unsurpassed.

Throughout the worlds in the ten quarters it prevails

Throughout means "universally," "extensively," "boundlessly." **Prevails** means that the Name spreads universally throughout the worlds in the ten quarters, countless as minute particles, and guides all to the practice of the Buddha's teaching. This means that, since there is no one—whether among the wise of the Mahayana or the Hinayana, or the ignorant, good or evil—who can attain supreme nirvana through his own self-cultivated wisdom, we are encouraged to enter the ocean of the wisdom-Vow of the Buddha of unhindered light, for his form is the light of wisdom. This form comprehends the wisdom of all the Buddhas. It should be understood that light is none other than wisdom.

Only those who say the Name all attain birth

Only those who means that only those who say the Name single-heartedly attain birth in the Pure Land of bliss; this is the meaning of "Those who say the Name all attain birth."

Avalokiteśvara and Mahāsthāmaprāpta come of themselves to welcome them

Namu-amida-butsu is the Name embodying wisdom; hence, when a person accepts and entrusts himself to this Name of the Buddha of inconceivable wisdom-light, holding it in mindfulness, Avalokiteśvara and Mahāsthāmaprāpta accompany him constantly, as shadows do things. The Buddha of unhindered light appears as Avalokiteśvara; he manifests himself as Mahāsthāmaprāpta. A sutra states that Avalokiteśvara, with the name Bodhisattva Treasure-response, reveals himself as the god of the sun and dispels the pitch darkness of ignorance in all beings; and Mahāsthāmaprāpta, with the name Bodhisattva Treasure-happiness, reveals himself as the god of the moon and illuminates the long night of birth-and-death. Together they bring forth wisdom in all beings.

Come of themselves to welcome: of themselves (*ji*) means "in person." Amida and a vast and numberless saintly host, consisting of innumerable manifestation-bodies of Buddhas, of Avalokiteśvara, and of Mahāsthāmaprāpta, appear in person to be alongside and always protect those who have realized true and real shinjin, at all times and in all places; hence the word "themselves."

Ji also means "of itself." "Of itself" is a synonym for *jinen*, which means "to be made to become so." "To be made to become so" means that without the practicer's calculating in any way whatsoever, all his past, present, and future evil karma is transformed into the highest good. To be transformed means that evil karma, without being nullified or eradicated, is made into the highest good, just as all waters, upon entering the great ocean, immediately become ocean water. We are made to acquire the Tathagata's virtues through entrusting ourselves to his Vow-power; hence the expression, "made to become so."[2] Since there is no contriving in any

---

2. The autograph version (see "Note on the Text," p. 112) reads: "Since, without his seeking it, the person who entrusts himself to the Buddha's Vow is made to attain all virtues and all good, it is said 'made to become so.' "

way to gain such virtues, it is called *jinen*. The person who has attained true and real shinjin is taken into and protected by this Vow which grasps never to abandon; therefore, he realizes the diamond-like mind without any calculation on his part, and thus dwells in the stage of the truly settled. Because of this, constant mindfulness of the Primal Vow arises in him naturally (by jinen). Even with the arising of this shinjin, it is written that supreme shinjin is made to awaken in us through the compassionate guidance of Śākyamuni, the kind father, and Amida, the mother of loving care. Know that this is the benefit of the working of jinen.

Come to welcome: come means "to cause to come to the Pure Land"; it is a word which expresses the actualizing of Amida's Vow, "If any should not be born in my land, may I not attain the supreme enlightenment." It indicates that a person is made to reject the defiled world and come to the true and real fulfilled land. In short, the word indicates the working of Other Power.

Come also means "to return." To return is to attain the supreme nirvana without fail because one has already entered the ocean of the Vow; this is called "returning to the city of dharma-nature." The city of dharma-nature is none other than the enlightenment of Tathagata, called dharmakaya, unfolded naturally. When a person becomes enlightened, we say he "returns to the city of dharma-nature." It is also called "realizing true reality or suchness," "realizing the uncreated or dharmakaya," "attaining emancipation," "realizing the eternal bliss of dharma-nature," and "attaining the supreme enlightenment." When a person attains this enlightenment, with great love and great compassion immediately reaching their fullness in him, he returns to the ocean of birth-and-death to save all sentient beings; this is known as attaining the virtue of Bodhisattva Samantabhadra. To attain this benefit is **come**; that is, "to return to the city of dharma-nature."

To welcome means that Amida receives us, awaits us. Hearing the inconceivable selected Primal Vow and the holy Name of supreme wisdom without a single doubt is called true and real shinjin; it is also called the diamond-like heart.[3] When sentient beings realize this shinjin, they attain the equal of perfect enlightenment and will ultimately attain the supreme enlightenment, being of the same stage as Maitreya, the future Buddha. That is, they become established in the stage of the truly settled. Hence shinjin is like a diamond, never breaking, or degenerating, or becoming fragmented; thus, we speak of "diamond-like shinjin." This is the meaning of **to welcome**.[4] The *Larger Sutra of Immeasurable Life* states: **When sentient beings aspire to be born in that land, then they attain birth, dwelling in the stage of non-retrogression. Aspire to be born in that land** is a command: All beings should aspire to be born in that land! **Then they attain birth** means that when a person realizes shinjin, he is born immediately. "To be born

---

3. We have followed the autograph version in this sentence. Our basic text has: "Hearing the revered Name of the inconceivable selected Primal Vow—the shinjin of supreme wisdom—and being without a single doubt is called true and real shinjin."

4. This sentence has been added in accordance with the autograph version.

immediately" is to dwell in the stage of non-retrogression. To dwell in the stage of non-retrogression is to become established in the stage of the truly settled. This is also called the attainment of the equal of perfect enlightenment. Such is the meaning of **then they attain birth.** **Then** means "immediately"; "immediately" means without any passage of time and without any passage of days.

That the Name spreads universally throughout the worlds in the ten quarters is due to the fulfillment of the Vow embodying the ocean of the One-Vehicle wisdom, the Seventeenth Vow of Bodhisattva Dharmākara's forty-eight great Vows, which states, "My Name shall be praised and pronounced by the countless Buddhas in the ten quarters." This is evident from the description of the Buddhas' witness and protection in the *Smaller Sutra.* The Buddhas' intention in their witness and protection is also expressed in the *Larger Sutra.* Thus, this Vow of compassion already shows that the Primal Vow, which encourages the saying of the Name, is the true cause of birth selected by Amida.

I have not gone into the significance of this passage as fully as I would like, but using these notes, please explore it carefully. It is the exposition of a master named Fa-chao, "the second Shan-tao." Tz'u-chio called him Master Fa-tao (Dharma Way), and in a biography he is called the Amida of Mount Lu-shan. He is also called Master Ching-yeh (Pure Karma). He was the reincarnation of the T'ang dynasty master Shantao of Kuang-ming Temple, and hence is known as "the second Shan-tao."

∽∞ ∽∞ ∽∞

That Buddha, in his bodhisattva stage, made the universal Vow:

When beings hear my Name and think on me I will come and welcome each of them,

Not discriminating at all between the poor and the rich and wellborn,

Not discriminating between the inferior and the highly gifted;

Not choosing the learned and those who uphold pure precepts,

Nor rejecting those who break precepts and whose evil karma is profound.

Solely making beings turn about and abundantly say the Name,

I can make bits of rubble change into gold.[5]

That Buddha, in his bodhisattva stage, made the universal Vow

That Buddha refers to Amida Buddha. **In his bodhisattva stage** indicates the time when Amida Buddha was Bodhisattva Dharmākara. **Universal** means "wide," "to spread." Bhikṣu Dharmākara established the supreme, unexcelled Vow and spread it widely. "Supreme" means that it goes beyond the vows of other Buddhas. It connotes "transcendent," "unequalled." The Tathagata's establishing of the universal

---

5. Quoted in *Essentials*, p. 60. From a hymn by Tz'u-min, included in *Hymns of the Nembutsu Liturgy in Fivefold Harmony*.

Vow is explained in detail in *The Essentials of Faith Alone*.

When beings hear my Name and think on me

Hear is a word indicating shinjin. **Name** refers to the Name embodying the Tathagata's Vow. **Think on me** instructs us, Hold this Name in mindfulness! This is implied in the compassionate Vow that all the Buddhas pronounce the Name. "Hold in mindfulness" means that people of true shinjin constantly recall the Primal Vow without interruption. *I will come and welcome each of them:* **Each of them** means "all inclusive," "everyone." **Welcome** means "to receive," "to await," expressing Other Power. **Come** means "to return," "to be made to come."[6] Thus, we are made to come and return to the city of dharma-nature. Since there is coming from the city of dharma-nature into this saha world to benefit sentient beings, **come** has the sense of "to come"; since there is attainment of the enlightenment of dharma-nature, it means "to return."

Not discriminating at all between the poor and the rich and wellborn

Not discriminating means "not choosing," "not rejecting."

---

6. We have followed the autograph version from this sentence to the end of the paragraph. Our basic text has: "**Come** means 'to return,' 'to come.' Thus, the Tathagata welcomes us and makes us return to the city of dharma-nature. Since the Tathagata comes into this world from the city of dharma-nature to benefit sentient beings, it also has the sense of 'to come.' In the *Larger Sutra* is the phrase, 'arising from suchness.' 'From suchness' means out of suchness. 'Arising' means to come forth."

Poor means "impoverished and in need." **At all** is for emphasis, meaning "not at all"; it also means "with" and "to lead." **Rich and wellborn** indicates the wealthy and the people of rank. Thus, without in the least differentiating among such people, Amida leads each and every person to the Pure Land.

Not discriminating between the inferior and the highly gifted

Inferior refers to those whose knowledge is shallow, limited, and slight. **Highly gifted** indicates those with great ability for learning. Amida does not choose between the two.

Not choosing the learned and those who uphold pure precepts

Learned means to hear and believe in numerous and diverse sacred teachings. **Uphold** means "to maintain." "To maintain" means not to lose or dissipate what we learn. **Pure precepts** indicates all the various Hinayana and Mahayana precepts— the five precepts, the eight precepts, the ten precepts of morality, all the Hinayana codes of precepts, the three-thousand regulations of deportment, the sixty-thousand regulatory practices, the diamond-like one-mind precepts of the Mahayana, the threefold pure precept, the fifty-eight precepts expounded in the *Brahma-net Sutra*, and so on—all the precepts for monks and for laymen. To maintain these is "to uphold" and to violate them is "to break." Even saintly people who observe these various Mahayana and Hinayana precepts can attain birth in the true fulfilled land only after they realize the true and real shinjin of Other Power. Know that it is impossible to be born in the true, fulfilled Pure Land by simply observing precepts, or by self-willed conviction, or by self-cultivated good.

Nor rejecting those who break precepts and whose evil karma is profound

Break precepts applies to people who, having received the precepts for monks or laymen mentioned earlier, break and abandon them; such people are not rejected. **Evil karma is profound**: evil people who have committed the ten transgressions or the five grave offenses, people of evil karma who have reviled the teaching or who lack seeds for Buddhahood, those of scant roots of good, those of massive karmic evil, those of shallow inclination to good, those of profound attachment to evil—such wretched men as these, profound in various kinds of evil karma, are described by the word **profound**. **Profound** means bottomless. Good people, bad people, noble and low, are not differentiated in the Vow of the Buddha of unhindered light, in which the guiding of each person is primary and fundamental. Know that the true essence of the Pure Land teaching (*Jōdo shinshū*) is that when we realize true and real shinjin, we are born in the true fulfilled land. **Come and welcome each of them** means making all beings of true and real shinjin return to the Pure Land by welcoming and leading them there.

Solely making beings turn about and abundantly say the Name

Solely making beings turn about instructs us, Singleheartedly make your heart turn about! **Turn about** means to overturn and discard the mind of self-power. Since those people who are to be born in the true fulfilled land are without fail taken into the heart of the Buddha of unhindered light, they realize diamond-like shinjin. Thus, they "abundantly say the Name." **Abundant** means "great" in the sense of great in number, "exceeding" and "supreme" in the sense of excelling and surpassing all good acts. This is because nothing excels the Primal Vow embodying Other Power. "To abandon the mind of self-power" admonishes the various and diverse kinds of people—masters of Hinayana or Mahayana, ignorant beings good or evil—to abandon the conviction that one is good, to cease relying on the self, to stop reflecting knowingly on one's evil heart, and further to abandon the judging of people as good and bad. When such shackled foolish beings—the lowly who are hunters and peddlers—thus wholly entrust themselves to the Name embodying great wisdom, the inconceivable Vow of the Buddha of unhindered light, then while burdened as they are with blind passion, they attain the supreme nirvana. "Shackled" describes us, who are bound by all our various blind passion. Blind passion refers to pains which torment the body and afflictions which distress the heart and mind. The hunter is he who slaughters the many kinds of living things; this is the huntsman. The peddler is he who buys and sells things; this is the trader. They are called "low." Such peddlers, hunters, and others are none other than we, who are like stones and tiles and pebbles.

I can make bits of rubble change into gold

This is a metaphor. When we entrust ourselves to the

Tathagata's Primal Vow, we, who are like bits of tile and pebbles, are turned into gold. Peddlers and hunters, who are like stones and tiles and pebbles, are grasped and never abandoned by the Tathagata's light.[7] Know that this comes about solely through true shinjin. We speak of the light that grasps because we are taken into the heart of the Buddha of unhindered light; thus shinjin is said to be diamond-like.

Although I have not set forth the meaning of this passage as fully as I would like, I have presented a rough explanation. I hope the reader will ask good teachers about its profound implications.

The passage is the exposition of Tz'u-min, master of the Tripitaka, who studied in India. In China he is known as Hui-jih.

∞ ∞ ∞

The land of bliss is the realm of nirvana, the uncreated;
Difficult is it, I fear, to be born there by doing various
good acts according to one's conditions.
Hence the Tathagata selected the essential dharma,
Instructing beings to say the Name of Amida with

---

7. In the autograph version, the passage corresponding to the preceding two sentences reads: "[This line] states that it is like tile and pebbles being made to become gold. Hunters, peddlers, and others are we, who are like stones and tile and pebbles. When we entrust ourselves without any doubt to the Tathagata's Vow, we are taken into the light that grasps, and without fail the enlightenment of great nirvana is made to unfold in us; that is, for hunters and peddlers, it is like stones and tiles and pebbles being made to become gold."

singleness, again singleness.[8]

The land of bliss is the realm of nirvana, the uncreated

Land of bliss is that Pure Land of happiness, where there are always countless joys and never any suffering mingled with them. It is known as the land of peace. It was Master T'an-luan who praised and called it "Land of Peace." Also, the *Treatise on the Pure Land* describes it as "the lotus repository world" and as the uncreated. **The realm of nirvana** refers to the place where one overturns the delusion of ignorance and realizes the supreme enlightenment. **Realm** means "place"; you should know it as the place of attaining enlightenment. **Nirvana** has innumerable names. It is impossible to give them in detail; I will list only a few. Nirvana is called extinction of passions, the uncreated, peaceful happiness, eternal bliss, true reality, dharmakaya, dharmanature, suchness, oneness, and Buddha-nature. Buddhanature is none other than Tathagata. This Tathagata pervades the countless worlds; it fills the hearts and minds of the ocean of all beings. Thus, plants, trees, and land all attain Buddhahood.

Since it is with this heart and mind of all sentient beings that they entrust themselves to the Vow of the dharmakayaas-compassion, this shinjin is none other than Buddha-nature. This Buddha-nature is dharma-nature. Dharma-nature is the dharmakaya. For this reason there are two kinds of

---

8. Quoted in *Essentials*, pp. 62–3. From Shan-tao's *Hymns of the Nembutsu Liturgy.*

dharmakaya in regard to the Buddha. The first is called
dharmakaya-as-suchness and the second, dharmakaya-as-
compassion. Dharmakaya-as-suchness has neither color nor
form; thus, the mind cannot grasp it nor words describe it.
From this oneness was manifested form, called dharmakaya-
as-compassion. Taking this form, the Buddha proclaimed
his name as Bhikṣu Dharmākara and established the forty-
eight great Vows that surpass conceptual understanding.
Among these Vows are the primal Vow of immeasurable light
and the universal Vow of immeasurable life, and to the form
manifesting these two Vows Bodhisattva Vasubandhu gave
the title, "Tathagata of unhindered light filling the ten
quarters." This Tathagata has fulfilled the Vows, which are
the cause of his Buddhahood, and thus is called "Tathagata of
the fulfilled body."[9] This is none other than Amida Tathagata.
"Fulfilled" means that the cause for enlightenment has been
fulfilled. From the fulfilled body innumerable personified
and accommodated bodies are manifested, radiating the
unhindered light of wisdom throughout the countless worlds.
Thus appearing in the form of light called "Tathagata of
unhindered light filling the ten quarters," it is without color
and without form, that is, identical with the dharmakaya-as-
suchness, dispelling the darkness of ignorance and un-
obstructed by karmic evil. For this reason it is called
"unhindered light." Unhindered means that it is not ob-

9. In the autograph version, this sentence reads: "This
Tathagata is called the fulfilled body. Because he has fulfilled his
Vow, which is the cause of his Buddhahood, he is called Tathagata
of the fulfilled body."

structed by the karmic evil and blind passion of beings. Know, therefore, that Amida Buddha is light, and that light is the form taken by wisdom.

Difficult is it, I fear, to be born there by doing various good acts according to one's conditions

According to one's conditions refers to turning the merit of practicing various good acts, which one performs according to one's own particular circumstances and opportunities, toward birth in the land of bliss. There are 84,000 gates of the dharma. Since they are all good practices done in self-power, they are rejected as not leading to birth in the true fulfilled land. Thus, **Difficult is it, I fear, to be born. Fear** means to be apprehensive; that is, apprehensive about whether a person can be born in the true fulfilled land through the adulterated good practices, the good practices characterized by self-power. **Difficult to be born** means that it is difficult to attain birth in the Pure Land.

Hence the Tathagata selected the essential dharma

Know that Śākyamuni Buddha selected the Name of Amida from among all the various goods and gave it to the evil beings, possessing wrong views and lacking faith, and living in this evil world of the five defilements. This is called **selected**, meaning "to pick out from among many." **Essential** means "wholly," "to seek," "to promise." **Dharma** indicates the Name.

Instructing beings to say the Name of Amida with singleness, again singleness

Instructing means "to preach," "the teaching." Here it refers to the instruction of Śākyamuni. **To say the Name** means to make a decision and not to calculate in any way. Thus, these words instruct us, Be wholehearted in the single practice of saying the Name embodying the selected Primal Vow!

With singleness, again singleness: the first **singleness** means that we should perform the single practice. **Again** means "furthermore"; it means "to repeat." Hence **with singleness** furthermore means "Be of one-mind!" That is, Be wholly of single practice and of one mind! Moreover, **singleness** means "one." "Wholly" implies, Do not be of two minds! Thus, not wavering in any way is one mind. Amida grasps, never to abandon, such a person of this single practice and one mind; therefore, he is called Amida. This is stated by Shan-tao, the master of Kuang-ming Temple.

This one mind is the shinjin of **leaping crosswise**. **Crosswise** means "across"; **leaping** means "going beyond." This way surpasses all other teachings, and through it one quickly goes beyond the great ocean of birth-and-death and attains supreme enlightenment; therefore the term **leaping** is used. It is made possible by the power of the Vow that embodies the Tathagata's great compassion.

The shinjin becomes the diamond-like heart because of Amida's grasp. This is the threefold shinjin of the Primal Vow of birth through the nembutsu and not the three minds of the *Meditation Sutra*. Bodhisattva Vasubandhu declares that this true and real shinjin is none other than the aspiration

45

to become a Buddha.　This is the great thought of enlightenment of the Pure Land.　This aspiration for Buddhahood is
none other than the wish to save all beings.　The wish to save
all beings is the wish to carry all beings across the great ocean
of birth-and-death.　This shinjin is the aspiration to bring all
beings to the attainment of supreme nirvana; it is the heart
of great love and great compassion.　This shinjin is Buddha-
nature and Buddha-nature is Tathagata.

To realize this shinjin is **to rejoice and be glad**.　People who
rejoice and are glad are called "people equal to the Buddhas."
To rejoice means to be joyous after being assured of attaining
what one shall attain; it is rejoicing after realizing shinjin.
To be glad means to always have joy uninterruptedly in one's
heart and constantly keep it in mind.[10]　It means **to leap and
jump**, expressing boundless joy: **to leap** is to dance to the
heavens, **to jump** is to dance on the earth.　The person who has
realized shinjin is also likened to the white lotus flower.

The difficulty of realizing this shinjin is taught in the *Larger
Sutra:* "To hear this sutra and maintain shinjin is the most
difficult among all difficulties;　nothing surpasses this
difficulty"; and in the *Smaller Sutra* we find, "It is the dharma
extremely difficult to accept."　But Śākyamuni Tathagata,
appearing in this evil world of five defilements, put this dharma
that is difficult to accept into practice and attained the supreme
nirvana.　He then gave this Name embodying wisdom to
the sentient beings living in defilement.　The witness of the

10.　The autograph version includes the following sentence:
"It means that after attaining what one shall attain, one rejoices in
both body and mind."

Buddhas throughout the ten quarters and the protection of the Tathagatas as numberless as the sands of the Ganges are solely for the sake of people of true and real shinjin. Know that Śākyamuni, our loving father, and Amida, our compassionate mother, guide us to shinjin as our own parents.

For vast ages in the past, under Buddhas who appeared in this world three times the sands of the Ganges in number, we awakened the great thought of enlightenment of self-power. Having performed good practices numerous as the sands of the Ganges, we are now able to encounter the karmic power of the great Vow. Those who have realized the threefold shinjin of Other Power must never disparage the other good practices or malign the other Buddhas and bodhisattvas.

ༀ   ༀ   ༀ

The person with the three minds will be born without fail in that land[11]

This means that because a person has the three minds he will be born without fail in that land. Thus Shan-tao states: *The person with these three minds necessarily attains birth. If the one mind is lacking, then he does not attain birth.*[12] **With these three minds** means that we must have the threefold mind. **If the one mind is lacking** means that no one can be born when this one mind is lacking. To lack the one mind is to lack shinjin. To lack shinjin is to lack the true and real threefold shinjin of the Primal Vow. To realize the three minds of the

---

11. Quoted in *Essentials*, p. 65. From the *Meditation Sutra*.

12. Quoted in *Essentials*, p. 65. From Shan-tao's *Hymns of Birth in the Pure Land.*

Meditation Sutra and then the threefold shinjin of the *Larger Sutra* is to realize the one mind. When this one mind is lacking, one is not born in the real fulfilled land. The three minds of the *Meditation Sutra* are parts of the mind of self-power of a person who pursues meditative and non-meditative practice. Know that the deep mind and sincere mind, which are means, are intended to bring the two goods—meditative and non-meditative—into the aspiration for the threefold shinjin of the *Larger Sutra*. When one has not attained the true and real threefold shinjin, one is not born in the true fulfilled land. Since one is not born, it is said **then he does not attain birth**. **Then** means "immediately." **He does not attain birth** means that he is not born. The person of mediative and non-meditative good acts—performing sundry practices, undergoing disciplines, and lacking threefold shinjin—will be born in the true and real fulfilled land, after countless lives in vast ages, after he has realized the threefold shinjin of the *Larger Sutra*. Thus, he is not born. The sutras state that even if such a person attains birth in the palace of womb or the borderland, he must pass five hundred years there; furthermore, out of millions upon millions of beings, scarcely a single one will advance to the true fulfilled land. Thus, we must carefully understand the importance of threefold shinjin and aspire for its realization.

∞ ∞ ∞

We should not express outwardly signs of wisdom, goodness, or diligence

People who aspire for the Pure Land must not behave

outwardly as though wise or good, nor should they act as though diligent.   The reason is stated, *for inwardly we possess that which is empty and transitory.*[13]   **Inwardly** means "within"; since the mind contains blind passion, it is empty and transitory. **Empty** means "vain," "not real," and "not sincere."   **Transitory** means "provisional," "not true."   For this reason, in the Tathagata's teaching this world is called the defiled world of the corrupt dharma.   All beings lack a true and sincere heart, mock teachers and elders, disrespect their parents, distrust their companions, and favor only evil; hence, it is taught that everyone, both in secular and religious worlds, is possessed of "Heart and tongue at odds," and "Words and thoughts both insincere."   The former means that what is in the heart and what is said are at variance, and the latter means that what is spoken and what is thought are not real.   Real means "sincere."   People of this world have only thoughts that are not real, and those who wish to be born in the Pure Land have only thoughts of deceiving and flattering.   Even those who renounce this world have nothing but thoughts of fame and profit.[14]   Hence, know that we are not good men, nor men of wisdom; that we have no diligence, but only indolence, and within, the heart is ever empty, deceptive, vainglorious, and

---

13.   "Do not express...empty and transitory" is quoted as a single sentence in *Essentials*, p. 66.   From Shan-tao's *Commentary on the Meditation Sutra.*

14.   The autograph version includes the following sentence: "This shinjin is the true seed, the true fruit, of the Pure Land; it is no lie or deception that this is shinjin that is the seed for [birth in] the true fulfilled land."

flattering. We do not have a heart that is true and real. *Reflect on this*[15] means that a person must understand this in accordance with the way things truly are.

∽∽   ∽∽   ∽∽

Nor rejecting those who break precepts and whose evil karma is profound[16]

This means that men who break the various precepts and whose evil karma is deep are not rejected. This was explained fully above. Please read the explanation carefully.

∽∽   ∽∽   ∽∽

If sentient beings, saying my Name up to ten times, do not attain birth, may I not attain the supreme enlightenment.[17]

This is from the text of the selected Primal Vow. It means that if the people who say the Name as stated in the Vow, "up to ten times," are not born in my land, may I not become a Buddha. **Up to** contains all the meanings of "upper or lower limit," "more or less," "near or far," "long continued." This is the Vow that Bodhisattva Dharmākara made in advance out of compassion for beings of later ages, seeking to end attachment to either many-calling or once-calling. We should be truly happy about this, and take delight and rejoice.

---

15. A term found in *Essentials*, p. 66.

16. This line from a hymn explained above (p. 39) appears again in *Essentials*, p. 60.

17. Quoted in *Essentials*, p. 69.   From the *Larger Sutra*.

ოჳ   ოჳ   ოჳ

Neither accommodated nor real[18]

This is a teaching of the Tendai school.   It has nothing to do with Shin Buddhism, and expresses the thought of the Path of Sages.   It is not the way of easy practice, so please ask people of the Tendai school about it.

ოჳ   ოჳ   ოჳ

If you cannot think on Amida[19]

This is the teaching which urges the person guilty of five grave offenses and ten transgressions and of engaging in defiled expositions of the dharma, "If you are tormented by suffering due to illness and cannot think on Amida, then simply say namu-amida-butsu with your lips."   This demonstrates that Amida made verbal utterance the essence of the Primal Vow. The expression *Say the Name of the Buddha of immeasurable life* refers to this fact, and **say** instructs us to utter the Name.

ოჳ   ოჳ   ოჳ

When you say namu-muryōju-butsu [namu-amida-butsu] ten times, because you say the Buddha's Name, with each utterance the evil karma of eight billion kalpas of birth-and-death is eliminated.[20]

The person who commits the five grave offenses is burdened

---

18.   A term found in *Essentials*, p. 69.

19.   This and the following phrase are quoted in *Essentials*, p. 70. Originally they form a single sentence of the *Meditation Sutra*.

20.   Quoted in *Essentials*, p. 70.   From the *Meditation Sutra*.

with evil karma, in fact, tenfold eight-billion kalpas of evil karma; hence, he is urged to say namu-amida-butsu ten times. It is not that the evil karma of tenfold eight-billion kalpas cannot be extinguished in a single utterance; but in this way, we are made to realize the seriousness of the evil karma of the five grave offenses. **Ten times** means that we should simply say the Name ten times with the lips. Thus, Shan-tao rephrases the selected Primal Vow, *If when I attain Buddhahood, the sentient beings in the ten quarters say my Name as few as ten times and yet are not born, may I not attain the supreme enlightenment.*[21] Here, in Amida's Primal Vow, **as few as** includes "few" in contrast to "many," teaching us that sentient beings who say the Name as few as ten times will without fail attain birth. Know that "thinking" and "voicing" have the same meaning; no voicing exists separate from thinking, and no thinking separate from voicing.

I have not explained the meaning of these passages as fully as I would like. Please ask good teachers about them, and with these notes explore their deep significance.

Namu-amida-butsu

That people of the countryside, who do not know the meanings of written characters and who are painfully and hopelessly ignorant, may easily understand, I have repeated the same things over and over. The educated will probably find this

---

21. Quoted in *Essentials*, p. 70. From Shan-tao's *Hymns of Birth in the Pure Land.*

writing peculiar and may ridicule it.   But paying no heed to such criticisms, I write only that ignorant people may easily grasp the meaning.

Shōka 1 (1257)   Eighth month   Nineteenth day
Written by Gutoku Shinran at eighty-five

THE ESSENTIALS OF
FAITH ALONE

BY SEIKAKU

When a person aspires to free himself from birth-and-death
and attain enlightenment, there are two routes open to him:
the gate of the Path of Sages and the gate of the Pure Land.
The Path of Sages consists of performing practices and accumulating merit while living in this saha world, striving to
attain enlightenment in this present life.   People who practice
the Shingon teaching aspire to rise to the stage of great enlightenment with their present bodies, and followers who
endeavor in the Tendai school seek to attain the enlightenment
known as "the stage of purifying the six sense organs" in this
life.   Although such indeed is the final objective of the teaching
of the Path of Sages, since the world has reached the age of the
corrupt dharma and entered the period of defilement, not even
a single person among millions can attain enlightenment in
this present life.   Hence, those who endeavor in the gate of
the Path of Sages in the present age become weary and

withdraw in their attempt to attain the enlightenment of becoming Buddha with this present body. In remote anticipation of the birth in this world of Maitreya, the Compassionate One, they look to the dawning sky 5,670,000,000 years in the future, or awaiting the appearance of even later Buddhas, they become lost in clouds of the night of countless transmigrations through innumerable kalpas. Or they merely yearn for the sacred sites of Vulture Peak or Potalaka Mountain where Avalokiteśvara dwells, or for the small reward of another birth as heavenly or human beings. Although any spiritual relationship with the Buddhist teaching is admirable, immediate enlightenment seems completely beyond hope. What is longed for remains within the three worlds, and what is hoped for is still life within transmigration. Why should they undertake much practice and cultivate understanding, seeking such a small reward? Truly, is it not the result of the dharma being too profound and our understanding too shallow, having become so far removed from the Great Sage, Śākyamuni?

Second is the gate of the Pure Land, in which, turning the merit of practice in the present life, one aspires to be born in his next life in the Pure Land to fulfill the bodhisattva practice and become a Buddha. This gate meets the needs of people of these latter days; it is truly a marvelous path. But this gate is itself divided into two: birth through various practices and birth through the nembutsu.

"Birth through various practices" means to aspire to be born in the Pure Land through observing filial piety toward one's parents, serving one's teacher and elders, maintaining the five precepts or eight precepts, and practicing charity and patience, and also through such practices as the Three Mystic Acts (Shingon) or the meditation exercise of the One Vehicle (Tendai). One may attain birth through these practices, for all are, without exception, none other than practices for birth into the Pure Land. But in all of them one aspires for birth by applying oneself relentlessly to practices, so they are called "birth through self-power." If the practices are done inadequately, it is impossible to achieve birth. They do not accord with Amida's Primal Vow; they are not illuminated by the radiance of Amida's grasp.

"Birth through the nembutsu" is to aspire for birth through saying the Name of Amida. Because this is in accordance with the Buddha's Primal Vow, it is called the act of true settlement; since one is pulled solely by the power of Amida's Vow, it is called birth through Other Power. If one asks why utterance of the Name is in accord with the Buddha's Primal Vow, we must recall the Vow's origin. In the distant past, before Amida Tathagata became a Buddha, he was called Bhikṣu Dharmākara. At that time there was a Buddha named Lokeśvara-rāja Buddha. When Bhikṣu Dharmākara had already awakened the thought of enlightenment, he desired to dwell in a land of purity and benefit sentient beings, and going before the Buddha he said: "Already I have awakened the thought of enlightenment and desire to establish a Buddha Land of purity. May the Buddha, for my sake, teach fully the innumerable, wondrous practices for adorning the Pure Land." Then Lokeśvara-rāja Buddha taught completely the good and bad of the human and heavenly beings in the pure lands of twenty-one billion Buddhas, as well as the coarse and the wondrous aspects of each of the lands, fully revealing each one of them. Bhikṣu Dharmākara listened and looked upon them, and discerning the bad he took up the good, casting out the coarse he aspired for the wonderful. He, for example, discerned and rejected lands which contained the three evil paths, but he requested and selected in his first Vow a world in which these three paths did not exist. We should understand that all his other Vows were established in this manner. Thus he chose the surpassing qualities from among the pure lands of twenty-one billion Buddhas and established the world of perfect bliss. It is as though cherry blossoms were made to bloom on the branches of willow trees, or those renowned sights, Kiyomi Beach and Futami Bay, were placed together. This selection was not made out of a brief consideration; it was the result of contemplation over the span of five kalpas. Thus, Dharmākara vowed to create a land most wondrous and adorned with purity, and he further contemplated: "The creating of this land is to guide all sentient beings. Though the land be exquisite, if it is difficult for beings to be born there, it would go against the intent of the great compassion and great vow. In seeking to determine the special cause for birth into the land of bliss, none among all the various practices is easily performed. If I were to select filial piety toward one's parents, those who lack piety could not be born; if I were to adopt the recitation of Mahayana sutras, the illiterate would have no hope; if I determined charity and observance of precepts to be the causal act, followers who are stingy and greedy or who break precepts would be dropped; if I made patience or effort the act resulting in birth, those given to anger or sloth would be completely abandoned.   The other practices are all likewise.   Hence, in order that all foolish beings, both good and evil, may equally be born and that they may all aspire for the land of bliss, I shall make simply the utterance of the three characters of the Name, *A-mi-da*, the special cause for birth therein."

Thus he completed five kalpas of profound contemplation and first of all established the Seventeenth Vow that all Buddhas shall say and praise his Name.   It is important to have a thorough understanding of this in regards to the Vow. Because he sought to guide sentient beings everywhere with his Name, he vowed that his Name be praised as the first step. If it were not so, since the Buddha has no desire for acclaim, what need would there be to be praised by all the Buddhas? Thus it is stated:

> The holy Name of the Tathagata is exceedingly distinct
>   and clear;
> Throughout the worlds in the ten quarters it prevails.
> Only those who say the Name all attain birth;
> Avalokiteśvara and Mahāsthāmaprāpta come of
>   themselves to welcome them.[1]

Next he established the Eighteenth Vow, the Vow of birth through the nembutsu, in which he declared that he would guide even people of ten utterances.   When we carefully reflect upon it, this Vow is truly vast and profound.   Because

---

1.   For Shinran's explanation of this passage, see *Notes on 'Essentials of Faith Alone'*, p. 30.

the Name is composed of but three characters, it is easy to keep even for one as foolish as Śākyamuni's disciple Panthaka, and in its utterance, it makes no difference whether one is walking, standing, sitting or lying down; nor is discrimination made about time, place, or circumstance, nor is distinction made between householder and monk, man and woman, old and young, good and bad.   Who, then, is left out?   Thus it is stated:

> That Buddha, in his bodhisattva stage, made the universal Vow:
> When beings hear my Name and think on me I will come and welcome each of them,
> Not discriminating at all between the poor and the rich and wellborn,
> Not discriminating between the inferior and the highly gifted;
> Not choosing the learned and those who uphold pure precepts,
> Nor rejecting those who break precepts and whose evil karma is profound.
> Solely making beings turn about and abundantly say the Name,
> I can make bits of rubble change into gold.[2]

This is birth through the nembutsu.

Bodhisattva Nāgārjuna states in his *Commentary on the Ten Bodhisattva Stages*:

---

2. See *Notes*, p. 36.

In practicing the Buddha-way there is a path of difficult practice and a path of easy practice. The path of difficult practice is like going overland on foot; the easy path is like receiving a favorable wind upon the sea-lanes. The difficult path consists in seeking to attain the stage of non-retrogression within the world of the five defilements; the easy path consists of being born in the Pure Land by virtue of simply entrusting oneself to the Buddha.

The difficult path is the gate of the Path of Sages; the easy path is the gate of the Pure Land. Thinking to myself, it seems that those who enter the Pure Land gate and yet endeavor in various practices for birth are like those who ride on a boat on the sea-lanes, but not receiving favorable wind, push oars and expend their strength, going against the tides and forcing through the waves.

In this gate of birth through the nembutsu, moreover, two practices are distinguished: single practice and sundry practice. Single practice is to perform simply the one practice of the nembutsu, awakening the aspiration for the land of bliss and the faith of entrusting to the Primal Vow, never mixing any other practices whatsoever with it. To say the Name of Amida only and think wholeheartedly on this one Buddha, never upholding other formulas or thinking on other Buddhas and bodhisattvas, is called single practice. Sundry practice, while taking the nembutsu as primary, places other practices alongside it and includes other forms of good acts. Of these two, single practice is to be considered superior. The reason is as follows. If one already aspires wholeheartedly for the

land of bliss, why include other things besides contemplating
on the master of that land? Life like a flash of lightning, or
a dewdrop at daybreak, and body like the plantain or a bubble
—yet one seeks in a mere lifetime of religious practice to depart
immediately from one's long abode in the five courses. How
can one leisurely combine diverse practices? For securing
spiritual bonds with the Buddhas and bodhisattvas, one must
await the morning when one can make offerings to the Buddhas
as one wishes; for the essential principles of the Mahayana
and Hinayana scriptures, one must await the eve when all the
teachings will be illuminated. Aside from aspiring for the
one land and thinking on the one Buddha, there is no other
necessity. People who enter the gate of the nembutsu but
combine it with other practices are attached to their former
practice and have difficulty abandoning them. Those who
hold to the One Vehicle or practice the Three Mystic Acts do
not change their aspiration to attain birth in the Pure Land by
turning over the merits of such practices, wondering what
can be wrong with pursuing them together with the nembutsu.
Without endeavoring in the nembutsu of easy practice that
accords with the Primal Vow, meaningless is it to follow
various practices rejected by the Primal Vow. Thus Master
Shan-tao declared: "Among those who abandon the single
practice and incline toward the sundry, not one in a thousand
can be born; among those of single practice, a hundred in a
hundred, a thousand in a thousand, can be born."[3] It is said:

The land of bliss is the realm of nirvana, the uncreated;

---

3. From *Hymns of Birth in the Pure Land.*

Difficult is it, I fear, to be born there by doing various
good acts according to one's conditions.

Hence the Tathagata selected the essential dharma,

Instructing beings to say the Name of Amida with
singleness, again singleness.[4]

That which is rejected as "various good acts done according
to one's conditions" is the attachment to one's own former
practice. In serving as a retainer, for example, one should
serve one's lord, depend on him, and wholeheartedly be loyal
to him. However, suppose a person, while evidently serving
his lord, in addition harbors designs concerning an unfamiliar,
distant person and, having him meet his lord, seeks to be
well spoken of by him. Compared with serving directly,
which is superior and which inferior is clearly known. Being
of two minds and being of one mind are as vastly different as
heaven and earth.

Concerning this, someone asks: "Suppose there is a person
who practices the nembutsu, reciting it ten thousand times
each day, and aside from that does nothing but play all day
and sleep all night; and another person who says it ten
thousand times and afterward reads sutras and recites the
names of other Buddhas: which is superior? In the *Lotus
Sutra* is the phrase, 'By virtue of this sutra one is born in the
land of peace.' Can reading this sutra be the same as playing
and frolicking? In the *Yakushi Sutra* is found the guidance
of eight bodhisattvas. Thinking on Yakushi Buddha is
surely not like useless sleep. I still cannot understand praising

---

4. See *Notes*, p. 41.

one as single practice and rejecting the other as sundry practice."

In considering this matter over again now, single practice is still superior. The reason is that we are essentially foolish beings of this defiled world who experience obstacles in everything. Amida, observing this, taught the path of easy practice. One who plays and frolics all day is a person of great distraction and confusion. One who sleeps through the whole night is a person of great lethargy. All are consequences of blind passion, difficult to sunder and difficult to control. When playing has ended, say the nembutsu; when awakening from sleep, recall the Primal Vow. This does not violate the performance of single practice. To recite the nembutsu ten thousand times and afterward hold in mind other sutras and other Buddhas seems splendid upon first hearing, but who determined that the nembutsu should be limited to ten thousand times? If you are a person of diligence, then recite all day. If you take up the *nenju*-beads, then utter the Name of Amida. If you face an object of worship, then choose the image of Amida. Directly await Amida's coming; why depend on the eight bodhisattvas to direct your way? You should rely solely on the guidance of the Primal Vow. Do not struggle to undertake the exercises of the One Vehicle (Tendai). In the capacities of nembutsu practicers there are the superior, the ordinary, and the inferior. Those of superior nature constantly say the nembutsu both night and day; in what interval, then, can they turn their attention to other Buddhas? You should reflect on this deeply and not become entangled in distracting doubts.

Next, in saying the nembutsu, you should possess the three minds. With the simple saying of the Name, who cannot obtain the virtue of one or ten utterances? Nevertheless, those who attain birth are exceedingly rare, the reason being that people do not have the three minds. The *Meditation Sutra* states: "The person who possesses the three minds will be born without fail in Amida's land."[5] Shan-tao says in his commentary: "The person who possesses these three minds necessarily attains birth. If one is lacking, then he does not attain birth."[6] This means that if a person lacks one of the three minds, he cannot be born. Although there are many who say the Name of Amida in this world, rare are those who actually attain birth. Know that this is because they do not possess the three minds.

Concerning these three minds: first is the mind of sincerity; this is the true and real heart and mind. In entering the Buddha path, one must first of all have a sincere mind; if the mind is not sincere, it is impossible to advance. Amida Buddha in the past accomplished the bodhisattva practices and established the Pure Land; in doing this he awakened the sincere mind. Hence, if you desire to be born in that land, you must also awaken a sincere mind. As to this true and real heart and mind, one must abandon that which is untrue and unreal and manifest that which is true and real. Indeed, although we are without profound aspiration for the Pure Land, on meeting others we talk as though we have deep

---

5. See *Notes*, p. 47.

6. See *Notes*, p. 47.

aspirations. While being deeply attached within to fame and gain in this life, our outward show is a rejection of this world. While on the surface we act as though we have a good heart and are noble, we have within an evil heart and a self-indulgent heart. This is called a heart and mind which is empty and transitory, opposite of the true and real heart and mind. You should turn away from this and firmly grasp the true and real heart and mind.

A person who erroneously grasps this, saying that if all things are not as they seem to be they might as well be empty and transitory, exposes to others even what should be matters of reserve and shame, and, contrarily, invites the faults of self-indulgence and shamelessness. Concerning the true and real heart and mind, in seeking the Pure Land, rejecting this defiled world, and entrusting to the Buddha's Vow, one must have such a heart and mind. It does not necessarily mean to openly manifest shame or to make a show of one's faults. You should deeply reflect[7] on this in all circumstances and on all occasions. Shan-tao's commentary states: "Do not express outwardly signs of wisdom, goodness, or diligence, while inwardly possessing that which is empty and transitory."[8]

Second is deep mind, the mind of trust. You should first know the features of the mind of trust. The mind of trust is to have deep faith in people's words without doubting them. For example, suppose that a man whom one deeply trusts and of whom one has no cause for suspicion whatever tells you

---

7. See *Notes*, p. 50.
8. See *Notes*, pp. 48–9.

about a place which he knows well at firsthand, saying that there is a mountain here, a river there. You believe deeply what he says, and after you have accepted these words, you meet other people who say it is all false. There is no mountain and no river. Nevertheless, since what you heard was said by a person whom you cannot think would speak mere fabrication, a hundred thousand people might tell you differently but you would not accept it. Rather, you deeply trust what you heard first. This is called trust. Now, believing in what Śākyamuni taught, entrusting yourself to Amida's Vow, and being without any doubt should be like this.

There are two aspects concerning this mind of trust: the first is to believe oneself to be a foolish being of defiled karma, subject to birth-and-death, from incalculable kalpas past continuously sinking and continuously turning, without any condition that could lead to liberation. The second is to believe deeply and decisively that, since one does not doubt that Amida's forty-eight Vows grasp sentient beings, one rides on the power of that Vow and will without fail attain birth. People often say: "Not that I don't believe in the Buddha's Vow, but when I reflect on myself, I see that my karmic hindrances have accumulated greatly and that the appearance of a good heart is rare. My mind is ever distracted and single-heartedness is impossible to achieve. I am forever negligent and lack diligence. Although the Buddha's Vow is said to be profound, how can he possibly receive me? Such thoughts appear truly sensible; arrogance is not aroused and self-conceit non-existent. Yet there is the crime of doubting the inconceivable power of the Buddha. Does one know what power the

Buddha possesses, when he says that because of one's karmic evil it is impossible to be saved? Even those wrongdoers who commit the five grave offenses, because of ten utterances, attain birth in an instant; even more so those who never go so far as to commit the five grave offenses, and in merit far surpass that of ten utterances.

If karmic evil is deep, all the more aspire for the land of bliss. It is said: "Not rejecting those who break precepts and whose evil karma is profound."[9] If your good is slight, think even more on Amida. It is said: "With three utterances, with five utterances, the Buddha comes to welcome." Do not meaninglessly despise yourself, weaken your heart, and doubt the Buddha's wisdom, which surpasses conceptual understanding. Suppose that there is a man at the bottom of a tall cliff unable to climb it, but there is a strong man on the cliff who lowers a rope and, thinking to have the man at the bottom take hold of it, tells him he will draw him up to the top. However, he holds his arms back and refuses to take the rope, doubting the strength of the man pulling and fearing that the rope is weak. Thus it is altogether impossible for him to climb to the top. If he unhesitatingly followed the man's words, stretched out his hands and grasped the rope, he would be able to climb at once. It is difficult for people who doubt the Buddha's power and who do not entrust themselves to the power of the Vow to climb the cliff of enlightenment. One should simply put out the hand of trust and take hold of the rope of the Vow.

---

9. See *Notes*, p. 39.

The Buddha's power is without limits; even the person deeply burdened with karmic evil is never too heavy. The Buddha's wisdom is without bounds; even those whose minds are distracted and self-indulgent are never rejected. The mind of trust alone is essential. There is no need to consider anything else. When trust has become settled, the three minds are naturally possessed. When the entrusting to the Primal Vow is true and sincere, there is no heart empty and transitory. When there is no doubt in the expectation of birth in the Pure Land, there is the thought of turning over merit toward it. Hence, although the three minds seem to differ from each other, they are all included in the mind of trust.

Third is the mind aspiring to be born in the Pure Land through turning over merit. The term is self-explanatory; therefore, I need not explain it in detail. It is to turn over the merit of the three modes of action of the past and present and to aspire to be born in the land of bliss.

Next, the text of the Primal Vow reads: "If sentient beings, saying (*nen*) my Name up to ten times, do not attain birth, may I not attain the supreme enlightenment."[10] Concerning these ten *nen*, some people have doubts and state: "The person who has one thought (*nen*) of rejoicing in the *Lotus Sutra* reaches deeply to the ultimate truth which is neither accommodated nor real.[11] Why are the 'ten *nen*' of the Vow understood to be ten utterances of the Name?" To answer this question: in describing the nature of the people of the

---

10. See *Notes*, p. 50.
11. See *Notes*, p. 51.

lowest grade in the lowest rank, the *Meditation Sutra* states,
"Upon reaching the moment of death, a person guilty of the
five grave offenses and the ten transgressions and burdened
with all kinds of evil follows, for the first time, the encourage-
ment of a true teacher, barely says the Name ten times and is
born at once in the Pure Land." This does not at all mean
quiet contemplation or deep reflection; it is simply saying the
Name with the lips. The sutra states, "If you cannot
think . . . . "[12] This has the meaning of not thinking deeply.
It also states: "Say the Name of the Buddha of immeasurable
life."[13] This encourages us simply to say the Buddha Name.
The sutra states: "When you say namu-muryōju-butsu
(i.e., namu-amida-butsu; lit. "Buddha of immeasurable life")
ten times, because you say the Buddha's Name, with each
utterance the evil karma of eight billion kalpas of birth-and-
death is eliminated."[14] The words "ten times" mean simply
saying the Name ten times. You should understand the text
of the Primal Vow in this way. Master Shan-tao profoundly
realized this import and restated the Primal Vow: "If, when
I attain Buddhahood, the sentient beings in the ten quarters
say my Name as few as ten times and yet are not born, may I
not attain the supreme enlightenment."[15] The words "ten
times" signify reciting with the lips.

1. Next, some people also say, "The nembutsu at the
moment of death contains a profound virtue. Extinguishing

---

12. See *Notes*, p. 51.
13. See *Notes*, p. 51.
14. See *Notes*, p. 51.
15. See *Notes*, p. 52.

the five grave offenses in ten utterances is the power of the nembutsu at the moment of death. The nembutsu of ordinary times lacks such power."

Reflecting upon this: True, the nembutsu at the time of death is particularly excellent in virtue. However, it is necessary to understand this fully. When a person is about to die, a hundred sufferings come upon him and right-mindedness is easily disturbed. At such a time, how is it that thinking on the Buddha has great virtue? In thinking about this, when one is gravely ill, nearing the end, and one's life is in peril, it is easy for trust to arise naturally. In actually observing the habits of people, we see that when they are without troubles they do not put trust in doctors and diviners, but when severely ill they have full trust in them. If they say that the disease will be cured with a certain treatment, people believe that it will truly be cured, and they even swallow bitter medicine and even receive painful treatment. When they are told that they will live longer if they perform a certain ceremony, they spare no riches and expend their energies in ceremonies and prayers. Thus, because their attachment to life is deep, if they are told they can prolong it, they have profound trust. The nembutsu at the moment of death should be understood in this manner. When you feel that the final moment of life has come and that you will not live, the suffering of your next life suddenly appears—the fiery car of hell comes or tormenting demons fill your eyes. Thinking of evading such suffering and escaping from such terror, you hear about the attainment of birth through ten utterances from a true teacher; suddenly a profound, momentous mind of trust arises and you have no doubt whatever. Because the revulsion against suffering is strong and the desire for happiness keen, one immediately awakens the mind of trust upon hearing that birth into the land of bliss is imminent. It is like trusting a doctor or an exorcist upon hearing them say that life will be lengthened. If one is of this mind, even though it is not one's last moment—if the mind of trust is established—the virtue of each utterance in ordinary times is equal to the nembutsu at the moment of death.

2. Next, people often say: "Even if I entrust myself to the power of Amida's Vow and aspire to be born in the land of bliss, it is difficult to know my defiled karma from past lives. How can I attain birth so easily? There are a variety of karmic obstacles. "Succeeding" karma does not necessarily take effect during the life in which it was created, but in lives to come it may bear fruit. Thus, although we have received birth into human life now, we may possess the karma for the evil paths without our knowing. If the power of such karma is strong and brings about birth into the evil courses, will it not be difficult to attain birth in the Pure Land?

Although the sense of this is quite sound, such people are unable to cut the net of doubt and create deluded views by themselves. Karma, more or less, may be compared to a scale. It first tips toward the heavier weight. If the power of my karma for birth in the evil courses were strong, then I would not have been born into human life but would first have fallen into the evil paths. This much is clear from having already received birth into human life: though we may possess karma for evil courses, that karma is weaker than the observance of the five precepts which brought about our birth into human life. If this is so, such karma cannot obstruct even the five precepts; how could it obstruct the virtue of ten utterances? The five precepts are acts of defiled beings; the nembutsu is a virtue of undefilement. In the five precepts no help from the Buddha's Vow is found, but we are guided to saying the nembutsu by Amida's Primal Vow. The virtue of the nembutsu, moreover, is superior to even the ten precepts and surpasses all the good of the three worlds. How much more does it surpass the scant good of the five precepts? Evil karma does not obstruct even the five precepts, it can never be an obstacle to birth.

3. Next, people again say: "The attainment of birth by ten utterances by people guilty of the five grave offenses comes about through their past good. It is difficult to possess such past good. How can we attain birth?"

Here, too, it is because they are lost in the darkness of folly that they vainly entertain such useless doubts. The reason is that those full of past good will cultivate good in this life also and fear doing evil acts. Those scant of past good will prefer evil acts in this life and not perform good. We clearly know the good and bad of past karma from the way this life is led. We, however, lack a pure heart, so we know that our past good is minimal. But though our karmic evil is heavy, we do not commit the five grave offenses, and though our good acts are few, we deeply entrust ourselves to the Primal Vow. Even the ten utterances of someone guilty of the five grave offenses comes about through his past good. How could it be, then, that the saying of the Name throughout one's life is not

also due to his past good? How can we think that the ten utterances of someone guilty of the five grave offenses is due to
his past good, while our own saying of the Name throughout
a lifetime is through our past good which is shallow? A little
wisdom is an obstruction to enlightenment, so it is said; truly,
here is an example.

4. Next, some who follow the way of the nembutsu say:
"The essence of the path to birth in the Pure Land is a trusting
mind. Once this mind of trust has become settled, it is not
always necessary to recite the nembutsu. The sutra teaches:
'down to one utterance'; hence, one utterance is understood to
be sufficient. When one seeks to accumulate many utterances,
it is, on the contrary, a failure to trust in the Buddha's Vow."
Thus they greatly mock and gravely slander those who recite
the nembutsu, saying that they are people who do not truly
believe in the nembutsu.

These people first of all abandon all Mahayana practices in
the name of "single practice of the nembutsu," and then,
adhering to the doctrine of "once-calling," they stop saying
the nembutsu. This is the means the demons have used to
deceive the sentient beings of this latter age. In such explanations there are both good and bad points. In principle the
statement that one utterance suffices as the act for birth in the
Pure Land is perfectly true; nevertheless, it is going too far
to say that the accumulation of a large number of utterances
shows the lack of a trusting mind. It does show, however,
a lack of a trusting mind if one believes that one utterance is
insufficient and birth requires accumulating a great number
of utterances. Though one utterance suffices as the act for

birth, some may think that it is important to accumulate more and more merit while passing their days and nights, and so, if they say the Name, they recite it day and night, and the merit increases more and more and the cause for birth becomes even more determined. Master Shan-tao stated that as long as one is alive, one should constantly say the nembutsu. Are we to say such a person lacks trust? To dismiss him with ridicule would be wrong. "One utterance" actually appears in a passage of the sutra. Not to believe it is not to believe the Buddha's word. Thus, one should believe in the settling of birth with one utterance, and further continue saying the Name without negligence throughout one's life. This is the true meaning of the teaching.

Although there are many important doctrines concerning the nembutsu, they can be summarized in the preceding way. Some people who read this will surely ridicule it. Nevertheless, both belief and slander will become a cause for each one's birth in the Pure Land. With the pledges of friendship in this life—brief as a dream—to guide us, we tie the bonds for meeting before enlightenment in the coming life. If I am behind, I will be guided by others; if I go first, I will guide others. Becoming true friends through many lives, we bring each other to the practice of the Buddha-way, and as true teachers in each life, we will together sunder all delusion and attachment.

> Honored Śākyamuni, the teacher,
> Amida Buddha, compassionate mother,
> Avalokiteśvara, on the left,

Mahāsthāmaprāpta, on the right,
The great ocean of immaculate beings,
The ocean of the three treasures, throughout the
  dharma-realm:
Singleheartedly I think on your witness;
Pity and comfort me, and hear my prayer.

GLOSSARY OF
SHIN BUDDHIST TERMS

Amida Buddha (*amida butsu* 阿弥陀仏) Amida (*a-mita*), literally "immeasurable [life and light]," is the Buddha whose essence is dharma-body as compassionate means, characterized by form. The formless dharma-body, in order to awaken beings of blind foolishness to itself, "manifested form and announced a Name," appearing as Dharmākara Bodhisattva. This bodhisattva established and fulfilled the special vow to save foolish and evil beings and became Amida Buddha. While the other Buddhas help people who accumulate meritorious deeds, practice meditative activities, and perfect wisdom, Amida Buddha saves the being of blind foolishness and karmic evil through "form" (Primal Vow) and "Name" (nembutsu). That is, the person who realizes himself as being truly human (ignorant and evil) and becomes his foolish self attains Buddhahood by virtue of Amida.

Amida's coming at the moment of death (*rinjū raikō* 臨終来迎) In traditional forms of Buddhism, contemplation on various aspects of the Buddhas is an important spiritual exercise, and the appearance of a Buddha before one is a sign of entrance into profound meditation and contact with the realm of enlightenment. In Pure Land

Buddhism, the vision of Amida and a host of bodhisattvas at the moment of death held a similar significance, for it was believed that at death Amida would come to take the nembutsu practicer into the Pure Land. Up until Shinran's time, Amida's coming formed the central focus of religious aspiration for Pure Land Buddhists and the circumstances and frame of mind of a person's final moments were considered to be of crucial importance.

Being grasped and never abandoned (*sesshu-fusha* 摂取不捨) While the English translation lacks the precision and aptness of the original term, the primary meaning is that when a man attains shinjin, he is said to have been grasped by true compassion, and there is no possibility of his being abandoned or forsaken for he has gone beyond the realm of birth-and-death. Never being abandoned is also expressed as residing in the stage of non-retrogression. *Sesshu* (being grasped) is a dynamic term having several connotations: the active and unremitting pursuit of all beings, especially those who turn away from the Vow; the grasping of all beings without discrimination; and the inevitable act of taking each and every being completely into the heart of true compassion. Man cannot grasp the immensity of true compassion (because of selfworking); he can only be grasped by true compassion (which is true working).

Benefit (*riyaku* 利益) In the Buddhist tradition the consequences of the religious life brings benefits to both oneself and others. The bodhisattva ideal, for example, is succinctly expressed in the statement: "self-enlightenment and enlightenment of others, the ultimate fulfilling of the activity of enlightenment." One of the definitions of an enlightened being reads: "The perfect fulfillment of bringing benefits to self and others equally." Shin Buddhism inherits this position, but establishes two stages in the gaining of benefits: the immediate, worldly benefits received by a person of shinjin in this life, and the final, ultimate benefit realized beyond the bounds of birth-and-death. The latter has two aspects: the process of going to be born in the Pure Land (which is benefiting the self) at which point one immediately begins the process of returning to this samsaric world to save all beings (which is benefiting others), both made possible by the empowerment of the Primal Vow. This follows the mythic pattern of withdrawal and return but on a higher, religious plane where the experience of transcendence, called birth in the Pure Land, is central. The former are benefits gained by the person of shinjin here and now, in the midst of ordinary life; and they include (1) protection of unseen, divine powers, (2) possession of highest virtue, (3) transformation of evil into good, (4) protection of all the Buddhas in countless universes, (5) praises of all Buddhas, (6) constant protection by Amida's light, (7) experience of abundant joy, (8) acknowledging and repaying the Buddha's blessings, (9) constant manifestation of compassion in daily life, and (10) inclusion in the group of truly settled.

Birth (*ōjō* 往生) The literal meaning of the original term *ōjō* is "to go to be born." Traditionally it meant attaining birth in the Pure Land after death, so that in an ideal religious environment, one could receive the aid of the Buddha, attain the non-retrogressive stage, and ultimately realize perfect enlightenment. People living in the Latter Ages (*mappō*), separated from the Buddha and facing a period of chaos and corruption, felt that enlightenment was impossible, unless they were reborn in a better world. For Shinran, however, "birth in the Pure Land" did not mean going to some ideal place for an extended period of Buddhist training; the term meant that at the moment of death one immediately attains the supreme enlightenment, the liberation from the karmic bonds of birth-and-death to realize nirvana. The term also meant the experience of shinjin, here and now in this life, in which one enters the group of the truly settled, attains non-retrogression, and becomes equal to perfect enlightenment. Thus, the idea of going to be born in the Pure Land which had a single futuristic meaning in traditional thought came to have a dual connotation: an awakening in this life called shinjin, and supreme enlightenment at the moment of death, both made possible by the empowerment of the Primal Vow.

Birth-and-death (*shōji* 生死)   The Sino-Japanese translation of *saṃ-sāra*, which means "the stream of time from birth to death and death to birth." All unenlightened beings repeat the empty, meaningless cycle in countless lives, driven only by the agitations of greed, anger, and folly. The purpose of Buddhism is to attain liberation from such a hollow existence, becoming a being of wisdom and compassion, filled with that which is true, real, and sincere.

Blind passion (*bonnō* 煩悩)   A comprehensive term descriptive of all the forces, conscious and unconscious, which propel the unenlightened person to think, feel, act, and speak in such a way as to cause uneasiness, frustration, torment, pain, and sorrow mentally, emotionally, spiritually, and even physically for himself and others. While Buddhism makes a detailed and subtle analysis of blind passion, as evident in such terms as craving, anger, delusion, arrogance, doubt, wrong views, etc., fundamentally it is rooted in the fierce and stubborn clinging to the foolish and evil self that constitutes the basis of our existence. When we realize the full implications of this truth about our selves, we see that the human condition is itself nothing but blind passion. Thus, just to live life as an unenlightened being is to manifest blind passion at all times, regardless of what we may appear to be on the surface. But the one who realizes this, having exerted his highest efforts and having failed to lead a life that is true, real, and sincere, is the person who is the major concern of Amida's Primal Vow.

Borderland (*henji* 辺地)   This is synonymous with land of indolence, womb of Buddha Land, and castle of doubt, all describing the realms into which Pure Land Buddhists are born, but which lie outside the Pure Land. They are for those who still cling to self-power and who have yet to realize fully the shinjin of Other Power. Thus, they are born in the borderland, next to the Pure Land, or in the land of indolence where they continue to indulge themselves in self-gratifications, or in the womb of the Pure Land where they are enclosed within a limited vision as if contained within a womb, or in the castle of doubt where they are imprisoned in their own self-centered uncertainties.

Buddha's witness and protection (*shōjō-gonen* 証誠護念) An idea based upon Amida Buddha's Seventeenth Vow which reads: "If, when I attain Buddhahood, the countless Buddhas throughout the worlds in the ten quarters do not all say my Name in praise, may I not attain the supreme enlightenment." The countless Buddhas or enlightened beings who praise Amida are witnesses to the efficacy of the Primal Vow to save each and every being, they attest to the working of Amida Buddha as the most powerful and decisive cause of enlightenment. Not only are they witnesses, but they actively protect the person of shinjin so that no demonic interventions or worldly difficulties can obstruct the freedom of his life.

Calculation (*hakarai* はからい) The original term *hakarai* is used in two opposing ways: first, it literally means to calculate, contrive, lay down a plan, and have intentions regarding birth in the Pure Land. This is small-minded *hakarai*, called self-power, of which a person becomes free as one accepts the working of Amida's Primal Vow and lives in complete Other Power. Second, it is also the working of Other Power as it plans, conceives, arranges, designs, and works out the deliverance of each karma-bound being into freedom, peace, nirvana. To receive the working of Other Power and let it guide one's life is to live in the grand *hakarai* of the Buddha of Immeasurable Life and Immeasurable Light, no longer having the need to rely on small-minded *hakarai*. To experience this is to know shinjin, the entrusting of self to Amida's Primal Vow and letting go of self-power. *Hakarai* as human calculation and as Buddha's working are mutually exclusive; when one exists, the other does not. Thus, when Amida's grand working covers the horizon of human experience, human calculation disappears—this is the Shin Buddhist way of actualizing the ideal of non-ego or nonself (*anātman*). What should be clearly understood is that the negation of human calculation does not mean the negation of a person's will to live the highest human life or to strive for enlightenment; rather what is negated is the attachment to small-minded calculations, claims, and achievements arising from misguided egoism.

Compassionate means (*hōben* 方便) The Sanskrit original, *upāya*, means "coming near," "approaching," and in extension, "means," "expedience." Generally speaking, it has two usages in Buddhism: the method or practice by which a man can attain Buddhahood, and the skillful means which Buddhas use to teach and to guide sentient beings to enlightenment. In Shin Buddhism, compassionate means refers to the manifestation of ultimate reality, which is beyond time and form, in the world of relativities—that is, of the dharma-body as suchness in the realm of birth-and-death—so that it comes into the range of human comprehension and description. Thus, Amida, with his Primal Vow, his Name and his Land, is described as dharma-body as compassionate means, which makes possible the salvation and enlightenment of all beings. In this case, however, dharma-body as compassionate means is considered to be one with dharma-body as suchness, so that compassionate means are considered not secondary but essential in our entrance into the ocean of Amida's Vow and ultimate enlightenment. This term is also used to refer to the compassionate means, such as the practices described in the Nineteenth and Twentieth Vows, used by Amida to lead practicers of self-power to the shinjin of Other Power, which is beyond self-power.

Defiled world (*edo* 穢土) This world of unenlightened beings, characterized by inverted thinking and feeling, is in direct contrast to the Pure Land. The defiled world is traditionally described either as the three realms of desire, form, and formlessness, or the six spheres of transmigration, namely, hellish existence, "hungry" ghosts, beasts, fighting demons, human beings, and heavenly beings. Since the unenlightened must endure the sufferings in the six spheres as the consequences of his karmic past, this world is also called *shaba* in Japanese (from Sanskrit *saha*, meaning "endurance"). The motto of Heian period Pure Land Buddhism, made famous by Genshin, was "Reject the defiled world and seek the Pure Land." This suggested an irrevocable dualism between this world of suffering and the Pure Land, with the crucial juncture coming at the moment of death, when the faithful were received by the Buddha into his land. Shinran, however, understood this phrase existentially and nondualistically, emphasizing both the transcendence of samsaric existence in shinjin here and now, in the midst of conventional life, and the attainment of supreme enlightenment at death, which is the dying to the karmic self for the person of shinjin.

Dharma-body (*hosshin, dharmakāya* 法身) D.T. Suzuki explains this term:

Kāya meaning "the body" is an important conception in the Buddhist doctrine of reality. Dharmakāya is usually rendered "Law-body" where Dharma is understood in the sense of "Law", "organisation", "systematisation", or "regulative principle". But really in Buddhism, Dharma has a very much more comprehensive meaning. Especially when Dharma is coupled with Kāya—Dharmakāya—it implies the notion of personality. The highest reality is not a mere abstraction, it is very much alive with sense and intelligence, and, above all, with love purged of human infirmities and defilements.

The Dharmakāya is not the owner of wisdom and compassion, he is the Wisdom or the Compassion, as either phase of his being is emphasized for some special reason. We shall miss the point entirely if we take him as somewhat resembling or reflecting the human conception of man. He has no body in the sense we have a human body. He is Spirit, he is the field of action, if we can use this form of expression, where Wisdom and Compassion are fused together, are transformed into each other, and become the principle of vitality in the world of sense-intellect. (*The Essence of Buddhism*, Kyoto: Hōzōkan, 1948, p. 47)

According to Shin Buddhism, dharma-body has two aspects:

"dharma-body as suchness" and "dharma-body as compassionate means." Dharma-body as suchness is formless and nameless, transcending the capacity of the ordinary mind to apprehend or speak about it; therefore, it manifests itself in the form of dharma-body as compassionate means which, fulfilling the Forty-eight Vows, becomes Amida Buddha. Amida is described variously as the fulfilled body, reward body, recompensed body, etc., all pointing to the fulfillment of the countless requirements necessary for the salvation of all beings. In *Kyōgyōshinshō* Shinran quotes the following passage from T'an-luan's *Commentary on Vasubandhu's Treatise on the Buddha Land* in order to illuminate the relation between these two aspects of dharma-body:

Among Buddhas and bodhisattvas there are two aspects of dharmakaya: dharmakaya-as-suchness and dharmakaya-as-compassion. Dharmakaya-as-compassion arises out of dharmakaya-as-suchness, and dharmakaya-as-suchness emerges into human consciousness through dharmakaya-as-compassion. These two aspects of dharmakaya differ but are not separate; they are one but not identical.

Dharmākara Bodhisattva (*hōzō bosatsu* 法蔵菩薩) The bodhisattva who established the vow to save all sentient beings in the universe through the utterance of his name and who became Amida Buddha through its fulfillment. The Vow of Amida is, strictly speaking, Bodhisattva Dharmākara's. In the story of Dharmākara we see that Amida is not a static symbol of absolute truth, but the expression of the ever-active working of compassion that lies at the core of Mahayana Buddhism. This working of compassionate means of the ultimate reality, the dharma-body as suchness, is one of the phases of jinen. Shinran states: "Manifesting a form from this (formless) treasure ocean of suchness, calling himself Dharmākara Bodhisattva, and making the unhindered Vows as the causes, he became Amida Buddha; that is the reason he is called the Tathagata of the fulfilled body . . . . This Tathagata is the dharma-body as compassionate means; the dharma-body of compassionate means is that which manifested form and announced a name and makes sentient beings realize it. This is Amida Buddha" (*Ichinen-tanen mon'i*).

Diamond-like heart and mind (*kongō-shin* 金剛心) The diamond (*vajra*) is a favorite metaphor in Mahayana Buddhism for the bodhisattva's indomitable and indestructible wisdom, which nothing can destroy and which sunders all forms of evil, both within and without. In the Path of Sages this metaphor is used to express the great power of prajna, which acts at the last stage of the bodhisattva's practice to cut the deepest root of attachment to birth-and-death. In Shinran's teaching, it is used to indicate that the mind and heart of the person of shinjin is indomitable and indestructible, not because of our strong conviction, firm belief, or hardness, but because its essence is Other Power.

Enlightenment (*satori* さとり, *shōgaku* 正覚) The root of suffering is ignorance or *avidyā* which blinds man's perception of life as it is. Thus, the goal of Buddhism is to transform this ignorance into wisdom that sees things, including the self, as they truly are. The realization of wisdom is enlightenment or satori, also called awakening or attaining Buddhahood. The relationship of ignorance and wisdom parallels that of sin and salvation in other religions. In Shin Buddhism human existence is seen as being permeated with blind ignorance; hence, the source of the transformation from ignorance to wisdom comes not from within man but from without in the form of the Primal Vow of Amida. The Primal Vow effects the enlightenment of all beings which is experienced in two stages: in the realization of shinjin here and now in this life, man becomes equal to enlightenment (but not fully enlightened because of his karmic limitations); and at the moment of death, he attains complete and supreme enlightenment (having become freed of all karmic bonds—intellectual, emotional, and physical). But since enlightenment is not a static state but a dynamic becoming, the enlightened being comes back to the defiled world of karmic limitations to work for the freedom and emancipation of suffering beings.

Eighteenth Vow Among the forty-eight Vows of Amida Buddha found in the *Larger Sutra of Immeasurable Life*, revered by Pure Land Buddhists, the most significant is considered to be the Eighteenth Vow, because it manifests the working of true compassion committed to the enlightenment of each and every being. Hōnen called it the King of the Vows. It reads: "If, when I attain Buddhahood, sentient beings throughout the ten quarters, with sincere mind, joyful faith, and aspiration to be born in my land and saying my Name up to ten times, do not attain birth, may I not attain the supreme enlightenment; excluded are those who have slandered the dharma and committed the five grave offenses." Based upon a passage which testifies to the fulfillment of this Vow, Shinran interpreted the three crucial terms—sincere mind, joyful faith, and aspiration for birth—not as necessary requirements on the part of the practicer but rather as demonstrating the compassionate working of the Primal Vow reaching down to man. According to Shinran, sincere mind is the mind of Buddha, not that of man filled with ignorance, vanity, and untruth; this sincere mind enters the mind and heart of man, causing him to experience joyful faith and prompting him to aspire for birth in the Pure Land. Since all three arise from true compassion, Shinran summarized them into One-mind which he said is synonymous with Other Power. Thus, everything is the working of Other Power, a compassion so boundless and profound that it takes into itself the very person whom it censures, "excluded are those who have slandered the dharma and committed the five grave offenses."

Equal to Tathagatas (*shobutsu to hitoshi* 諸仏とひとし) Even though one is a being of karmic evil, when he entrusts himself completely to the Primal Vow, devoid of any form of self-willed calculation, his heart and mind is equal to those of Tathagatas. This is possible because this entrusting (shinjin) is none other than the heart and mind of Amida Buddha working in man. To express this, Shinran speaks of the heart and mind of a person of shinjin always being in the Pure Land, even though his body remains in this relative world of defilement. This should not be understood as implying any duality of body and mind, or that the mind, separating itself from the body, goes to a remote Pure Land.

Evil (*aku* 悪) Term used in contrast to good, implying (1) some awareness of what is good and what is evil, (2) the possibility of choosing one over the other, and (3) a sense of moral and individual responsibility. Thus, we find such frequent expressions as the following: favor only evil, choosing to do evil, doing evil throughout one's lifetime, awaken to evil, boast of evil, etc. Specific references to evil include the five great offenses and ten transgressions, but it is not limited to these categories only. The awareness of evil is an essential part of Buddhist life, but the term may be used in reference to a person without any moral or religious conscience. Ultimately, however, it is only when we are carried by the power of the Primal Vow, or experience true compassion in all its dimensions, that we come to know evil for the first time.

Five defilements (*gojoku* 五濁) Defilements or impurities which make this world of ours a difficult place in which to pursue Buddhist practices effectively for the sake of enlightenment. The five types of defilements which increase with time are as follows: defiled age (*kalpa*) when war, pestilence, famine, natural calamities, and pollution abound; defiled view (*dṛṣṭi*), characterized by confrontation of ideologies, confusion of values, and prevalence of nihilistic attitudes; defiled passion (*kleśa*), the flourishing of greed, anger, ignorance, and evil ways; defiled beings (*sattva*), an increase in human life of inferior quality, dull minds, weak bodies, and egotism; and defiled life (*āyus*), the vain wasting and shortening of human life. The five are intimately involved with each other: defiled age is caused by defiled views which arise from defiled passion controlling the lives of defiled beings who manifest defiled life.

Glossary

Five grave offenses (*go-gyaku* 五逆)　The early tradition lists them as: 1) killing one's mother, 2) killing one's father, 3) killing an arhat, 4) causing blood to flow from the body of a Buddha, 5) disrupting the harmony of the assembly of monks. Another tradition gives them as: 1) destroying stupas and temples, burning sutras and Buddhist images, or plundering the three treasures; causing others to do these acts; or being pleased at seeing them, 2) slandering the disciples and solitary-Buddhas or the Mahayana teaching, 3) harassing the practice of a monk or murdering him; 4) committing any of the five grave offenses of the early tradition, 5) committing the ten transgressions with the conviction that there will be no karmic recompense and without fear for the next life, or teaching others such an attitude.

Foolish being (*bombu* 凡夫)　One of the Sanskrit equivalents of foolish being is *bāla*, which has various connotations: immature, silly, stupid, foolish, ignorant. This term, however, is not to be understood in the conventional sense suggested by these words, for it is the result of a profound religious awakening in which even the so-called intelligent person, when illumined by Unhindered Light and brought to awareness by the wisdom of shinjin, comes to realize himself as a foolish being who is forever motivated by blindly self-centered desires, attached to the fascinations of this evanescent world, and unable to resolve the contradictions of human existence thoroughly. In fact, Shinran says that true wisdom is brought forth only from the heart and mind of the person who is awakened to himself as a foolish being. This awakening consists of two mutually opposing aspects: one is the realization of the foolishness and evilness of one's own being, and the other is the realization of the great compassion of Other Power. An arrogant and prideful person obstructs the working of the Primal Vow and never sees himself as a foolish being. A synonym for this term is "ignorant being" (*gusha*).

Fulfilled land; True and real land (*shinjitsu-hōdo* 真実報土)　A synonym for the Pure Land. It is a realm established by Amida Buddha, having fulfilled every necessary requirement for the enlightenment of all beings. Thus, it is a land which becomes manifest as the fulfillment of Amida's Vow, but at the same time it is the realm of man's ultimate fulfillment. Thus, in Shinran's thought Jōdo or Pure Land is none other than truth, reality and sincerity, which alone can fulfill man's deepest needs; rarely does he refer to it in terms of the traditional mythical references, such as the land of bliss or the Western land.

Giving and **being given** (*ekō* 廻向) The term *ekō* is impossible to translate fully into English but literally means "turning over," "redirecting," or "giving to another," traditionally rendered as "merit-transference." The concept of *ekō* was born in the bodhisattva tradition in which religious practices are undertaken for the benefit not only of oneself but of others also. The deep wish or vow of the bodhisattva is for the spiritual and moral elevation of all beings, traditionally expressed as "going out from birth-and-death." Therefore, it is only natural that he share his accomplishments with others. This sharing or turning over, however, does not involve any form of sacrifice, as might be presumed, for it is an act of compassion performed in non-dichotomous thinking and feeling.

In other schools of Buddhism, then, *ekō* signifies a practicer's directing of merit towards his own and others' attainment of enlightenment, and in traditional Pure Land Buddhism, which confronted practically the tremendous difficulties of the bodhisattva path, *ekō* came to mean the directing of one's inadequate merits not towards others but towards the attainment of birth in the Pure Land, where one could realize enlightenment and then return to this world to work for the salvation of all beings. Shinran, however, viewed *ekō* from the opposite perspective and used the term to signify the Enlightened One's (Amida Buddha's) directing and giving his merits to practicers. Thus, the nembutsu—and shinjin as its realization by us—are said to be given by Other Power.

Shinran speaks of two kinds of turning over: outgoing *ekō* (i.e.

outward from birth-and-death) which effects man's birth in the Pure Land, and returning *ekō* (into birth-and-death) which enables him to come back into this defiled world for the salvation of all beings. Both activities are manifestations of the working of Amida, that is, of what is given by Amida.

Hearing (*mon* 聞) Hearing or listening to the teaching has been central to the Buddhist path; for example, in the cultivation of prajna the earlier stages are to be pursued by hearing (*śruta*), reflecting (*cintā*), and practicing (*bhāvanā*) what one has heard. The act of hearing is also said to implant the seed of subconscious influence which will ultimately bear rich fruit. In Shin Buddhism, however, hearing is not just the beginning; it is the alpha and omega of religious life, for ultimately what is heard defines what one is, the complete identification being none other than the experience of shinjin. This is to say, "hearing" is to help us in "awakening" to (1) Amida's Primal Vow as the highest expression of compassion in relation to (2) the deep crisis of one's existential plight. Thus, "hearing" and "awakening" are experienced in double exposure. Religiously speaking, hearing is to hear the call of true and real life to return to the home of homes, and awakening is to respond with one's whole being to that call and follow the call until one has arrived home. This call is Namu-amida-butsu.

Ignorance (*mumyō* 無明) The inability to see reality as it is, an ignorance deeply entrenched in human existence itself. The root of all kinds of delusion and suffering, as exemplified by *avidyā*, the basic factor in the twelve cycle of causation or the three poisons of greed, anger, and ignorance. The goal of Buddhism is to transform ignorance into enlightenment in which one sees things, including the self, as they truly are.

In Shin Buddhism, the true realization of oneself as foolish—as a person of *avidyā*—comes about only through the working of the nembutsu or shinjin, and so is called the "wisdom of shinjin" or the "nembutsu of wisdom." This wisdom is knowledge of oneself as ignorant; hence, it is wisdom that takes ignorance as its basis. When the ignorant person attains this wisdom, his ignorance, rather than being done away with, is transformed into wisdom.

Jinen (*jinen* 自然) A term for the ultimate reality of Buddhism, expressing suchness, or things-as-they-are, free from the bondage of birth-and-death. Jinen thus signifies that which is beyond form and time, and beyond the domain of human intellect and efforts. It is, in other words, dharma-body as suchness, which "fills the hearts and minds of the ocean of all beings" (*Notes*, page 42). To awaken to this dharma-body as suchness is to become Buddha.

It is impossible for man to realize dharma-body as suchness through human calculation; however, it works in man as the body as compassionate means to make itself known. This working is also called jinen by Shinran, and with this intention he explains the meaning of jinen as, "It is not through the practicer's calculation; one is made to become so."

Although other forms of Buddhism speak of "attaining the Buddhahood of dharma-body as suchness with the present body," Shin Buddhism, recognizing the nature of man's condition as a living being, places complete attainment with birth in the Pure Land of the dharma-body of compassionate means at death. However, jinen works in man constantly, and to experience and awaken to this working—i.e. to realize shinjin—is also a kind of attainment. Shinran calls it "the dawning of the long night of ignorance." Thus, when Shinran says that "from the very beginning one is made to become so," "becoming so" can be viewed in terms of several aspects of a process.

Jinen, as Amida's Vow, works "to have each person entrust himself [to the Vow] in namu-amida-butsu and be received in the Pure Land; none of this is through the practicer's calculation." That is, it brings us to the realization of shinjin, and this means that we attain the stage of non-retrogression. Concerning this realization of shinjin, Shinran states, " 'To be made to become so' means that without the practicer's calculating in any way whatever, all his past, present, and future evil karma is transformed into the highest good (Buddha's virtues)" (*Notes*, page 32).

Further, the person of shinjin is necessarily born in the Pure Land. This also is the working of jinen. To attain birth in the case of Shinran means to realize supreme nirvana, and he speaks of it as "returning to the city of dharma-nature." Indeed, it is to become the supreme Buddha. Thus, "when a person attains this enlightenment, with great love and great compassion immediately reaching their fullness in him, he returns to the ocean of birth-and-death to save all sentient beings" (*Notes*, pages 33~4).

From the standpoint of the practicer, jinen—the working of the Primal Vow—means the negation of all calculation. The negation of calculation means that he is saved through jinen without freeing himself from blind passion.

Karmic evil (*akugō* 悪業) This term indicates all human acts of daily life—thought, speech, and conduct—which, being defiled by blind passion and by unconscious ignorance harbored in the depths of one's being, invite suffering. The term is frequently used together with ignorance (*mumyō-akugō*) and blind passion (*bonnō-akugō*), pointing to the deep roots of karmic evil in samsaric existence itself. In fact, because of eons of repetition and habit, karmic evil is so entrenched in human life that it is virtually impossible to become free of its adverse consequences by ordinary moral effort or conventional religious practices. A related term which we have translated as "evil karma" (*tsumi, zaigō*) connotes even more clearly the beginningless origin of unenlightened, samsaric life which makes us the foolish beings we are. Evil karma contributes to the two greatest evils in Buddhism: slandering the Buddha's teaching which rules out any possibility of enlightenment, and doubting the Buddha's wisdom which strengthens self-sufficient arrogance and hence chains us to samsara. Yet both karmic evil and evil karma are the the major concerns of Amida's salvific power contained in the Primal Vow which will not rest until they are transformed into the contents of enlightenment.

Leaping crosswise (*ōchō* 横超) A term used by Shinran to describe the instantaneous attainment of enlightenment by virtue of the Primal Vow, contrasting it to the progressive stages of evolution over long periods of time required for attaining enlightenment in paths other than nembutsu. Shinran writes, "In the space of one moment, quickly and immediately, one leaps and attains the supreme true enlightenment. Thus, it is called leaping crosswise" (*Kyōgyōshinshō* SSZ II, 73).

Light (*kōmyō* 光明) Light is said to be the concrete manifestation of wisdom. In the opening lines of the Chapter on True Faith in *Kyōgyōshinshō*, Shinran states that the essence of the Buddha is Inconceivable Light and that of the Pure Land is Immeasurable Light. This makes clear the fact that Shinran is not positing an objective being called Buddha who emits rays of light or an objective realm called Pure Land which shines forth with light; what he is saying is that Light (or wisdom and, in extension, compassion) is the very essence and reality of Buddha and Pure Land. What this means in the actual life of the person of shinjin is that he is nurtured by an invisible power conceived as Light which (1) penetrates through the hard crust and dark mass of his blind passion, (2) melts by its warmth the mass of blind passion hardened through aeons of aimless wandering, and (3) nourishes a new being and new life. Thus, Shinran praised the wondrous working of Light variously and called Amida Buddha by such names as Immeasurable Light, Illimitable Light, Unhindered Light, Incomparable Light, Majestic Light, Immaculate Light, Joyful Light, Wisdom Light, Incessant Light, Indescribable Light, and Light More Luminous than the Sun and Moon.

Maitreya (*miroku* 弥勒) The future Buddha, now residing in Tushita heaven, who will appear as the next Buddha in our world 5,670,000,000 years hence. Maitreya has put forth immense effort, unimaginable sacrifices, and endured demanding religious practices to achieve the status of the next Buddha. The person of shinjin is likened to Maitreya, for he too will become a Buddha in the next life, but he of course does not undergo the disciplines required of Maitreya for everything has been accomplished for him by Amida Buddha.

Mindfulness (*okunen* 憶念) The original Sanskrit, *anusmṛti*, means to hold or keep in mind, recollect, remember, etc., but in Shin Buddhism it is used in two ways: first, as an equivalent of shinjin itself: and second, as always remembering, consciously or unconsciously, the working of Amida as the natural consequence of the Primal Vow directed to the foolish being.

Mind of Enlightenment (*bodaishin* 菩提心) A basic requirement of the Mahayana bodhisattva is the awakening of the mind or thought of enlightenment (*bodhicitta*) which is not mere resolution of will or a decisive commitment to the Buddhist path, but a radical change of life direction, originating from a new center of energy, in fact, from the heart of enlightenment itself. When the dormant religious aspiration has been awakened, nothing can stop the person from reaching final and supreme enlightenement. In Shin Buddhism, however, the ordinary person is considered incapable of arousing such an aspiration; therefore, the term is used as a synonym of true compassion and true love, that is, the heart and mind of Amida. When the heart and mind of Amida enters the mind of man to become shinjin, for the first time a person realizes the mind of enlightenment in shinjin.

Name (*myōgō* 名号, *nembutsu* 念仏) The Sanskrit original, *nāmadheya*, simply means the "name" of a Buddha or bodhisattva, but it has a special significance in Shin Buddhism; hence the capital letter. It might be said that "Amida Buddha" is a name, but namu-amida-butsu is the Name. The difference between the two is that the Name includes "namu" as a necessary and essential component. "Namu" is being called and invited to the Pure Land by Amida. It means that one is made to entrust oneself completely to the

Primal Vow of Amida fulfilled for one's own sake. "Namu," therefore, is a crucial part of the enlightenment realized by Amida Buddha, and its inclusion in the Name reveals the absolute nature of Amida's compassion. Thus, when the Name is said, it is neither a petitionary prayer nor a magical formula, but the call of Amida and man's realization of that call. In other words, when the Name which is filled with Amida's profound wish for man works on him and becomes a reality in shinjin, it flows forth as namu-amida-butsu. Here there is no room for any form of doubt, hesitation, or self-willed calculation.

Nembutsu (*nembutsu* 念仏) This term has several meanings in the history of Buddhism, based on the various connotations of *nen* (meditating, thinking, pronouncing, etc.): meditating on the special features of the Buddha image, holding to the thought of the Buddha, and pronouncing the name of a Buddha. In Shin Buddhism nembutsu has two meanings: it is the Name (*myōgō*) as the ultimate manifestation of true compassion, and it is the saying of this Name, *namu-amida-butsu*.

Non-retrogression (*futaiten* 不退転) The realization of shinjin means that one has entered the ocean of Amida's Primal Vow, so that "the long night of birth-and-death has already dawned." This is also expressed as "being grasped by Amida never to be abandoned" and as entering the community of the truly settled. Shinran calls this the stage of non-retrogression (*avaivartika*), a term originally used to describe the bodhisattva on the path of enlightenment who will never backslide because he has realized suchness non-dichotomously—i.e. has already reached the other shore of nirvana—even though he lives in a dichotomous world.

Once-calling and Many-calling (*ichinen-tanen* 一念多念) Centered around the term *nen* which can mean either "uttering" the Name of Buddha or "thinking" on the Buddha, a conflict arose between the advocates of once-calling and many-callings. Originally, it began as the question of the sufficiency of a single calling of nembutsu, namu-amida-butsu, based upon the saving power of Amida, or the necessity of frequent saying of nembutsu, for the practice of Pure Land path was recitative nembutsu; but later it became a debate about stressing the experience of shinjin which requires only a single uttering or emphasizing constant mindfulness which means multiple recitation of nembutsu. For Shinran, however, both are valid, having their origins in the Primal Vow, and selecting one at the expense of the other is to make it a product of calculation which no longer accords with the Primal Vow. In fact, they do not stand in opposition but are mutually inclusive, because whether mental (shinjin) or physical (reciation), they are not the practicer's but Amida's working. It is impossible to render *nen* with its multiple meanings into English, but for our purposes we have translated it as "calling," since it connotes not only recitation but also the source and contents of nembutsu, which is a call from Amida and our response to it. When the "calling" involves our whole being, we experience shinjin in which time and timelessness converge.

Oneness (*ichinyo* 一如) Fundamental reality in Buddhism, synonymous with dharma-nature, true reality, suchness, Buddha-nature, nirvana, etc. Oneness does not mean the submersion of differences or loss of distinctions, as frequently misunderstood; rather, the opposite phenomenon is seen where each thing or being stands out in its individual uniqueness, yet there is an orchestrated harmony and unity. That is, oneness is based upon the suchness of each reality shining forth in its own, individual radiance.

One-mind (*isshin* 一心) A synonym of shinjin, the manifestation of the working of Other Power. The locus classicus is Vasubandhu's statement, "O Bhagavat, with single-heartedness I take refuge in the Tathagata of unhindered light filling the ten quarters." "Single-heartedness" (adverb) may also be translated as "One-mind" (noun), the original being *isshin* for both. One-mind means that a person is single-minded, free of doubt, and not wavering between choices;

it is none other than Other Power. When One-mind is analyzed, it becomes the threefold shinjin of the Eighteenth Vow. Shinran also states that One-mind is the aspiration for Buddhahood which is none other than the quest for the salvation of all beings, thus showing that shinjin results in the dual benefit which comes to self and others.

One Vehicle (*ichijō* 一乘) Vehicle (*yāna*) refers to the teaching, as in the parable of the raft, which must be actually utilized to go beyond birth-and-death. It is not an object of contemplation or philosphical study. In Mahayana Buddhism reference is made to the Three Vehicles, including the gradations of the way of disciples (*śrāvaka*), solitary awakened ones (*pratyekabuddha*) and bodhi-sattvas, and to the One Vehicle which is non-exclusive and makes no such distinctions. Shinran, however, went beyond them and speaks of the One Buddha Vehicle of the Primal Vow or the Ocean of the One Vehicle of the Primal Vow, meaning that it is only through the power of the Primal Vow, or synonymously by entering the ocean of the Primal Vow, can one attain the supreme enlighten-ment. In *Notes on 'Essentials of Faith Alone'* Shinran states, "Since there is no one—whether among the wise of the Mahayana or the Hinayana, or the ignorant, good or evil—who can attain supreme nirvana through his own self-cultivated wisdom, we are encouraged to enter the ocean of the wisdom-Vow of the Buddha of unhindered light" (page 31).

Other Power (*tariki* 他力) This is the power of the Vow of Amida, which transforms ignorance into wisdom, darkness into light, and evil into virtue. The "Other" here is not a term relative to "self" but an Absolute Other which is beyond all sentient beings, working within and without each self to effect his enlightenment. In the words of Shinran, "Other Power means to be free of any form of calculation" (*Letters of Shinran*, Letter 10). This means that Other Power is to be realized where all selfworking has ceased and one has been grasped by true compassion.

Path of Sages (*shōdō-mon* 聖道門)   This term indicates the schools
of Buddhism which are basically monastic, such as Zen, stressing
the observance of precepts, including celibacy, dietary restrictions,
rules of conduct, etc., and the pursuit of formalized methods of
religious practice, meditative and non-meditative, in order to attain
supreme Buddhahood.   In constrast to this path is the Pure Land
path, which finds its way to becoming the supreme Buddha through
being born in the Pure Land.   In the former, one expects to become
enlightened in this world, whereas in the latter one attains enlightenment in the Pure Land after death.

Practicer (*gyōja* 行者)   This slightly unusual English word has been
employed to translate an expression frequently used by Shinran,
shinjin no gyōja (practicer of shinjin) or *nembutsu no gyōja* (practicer
of nembutsu), to emphasize the fact that the arena of religious
practice for a Shin Buddhist is everyday life, involving duties and
responsibilities, personal and social entanglements, emotional and
physical agitations, and all of the problems that arise from trying to
lead the highest life of good.   Stated conversely, shinjin and nembutsu in fact constitute the only practice by which those who are
involved in everyday life and unable to undertake monastic practice
can free themselves from birth-and-death and attain Buddhahood.

Precepts (*kai* 戒)   Precepts or *śīla* is one of the Three Learnings,
along with meditative practice and wisdom.   In later Buddhism a
great variety of precepts were established, but they all had one basic
purpose: to cultivate self-discipline, purge distractions, and sharpen
critical thinking.

Primal Vow (*hongan* 本願)   A vibrant life-force which makes
sentient beings attain supreme enlightenment works in each being.
It appeared in the person of Śākyamuni, who was moved to expound
the *Larger Sutra*, revealing for the first time in history this life-force
as the Primal Vow of the Buddha of Immeasurable Life and Light.
But the Sanskrit original, *pūrva-pranidhāna*, implies that the Primal

Vow existed prior to (*pūrva*) the earliest being, and that it is the basis and foundation of each being, leading it to its self-awareness from the bottomless depth, that is, from dharma-body as suchness. In other words, the Primal Vow is the working of Amida Buddha (dharma-body as compassionate means) issuing forth as the profound desire, wish, or prayer from the deepest source of life itself, to free all beings from the weight of karmic evil in the ocean of birth-and-death. It is the manifestation in time, from ten kalpas ago, of that which is timeless.

This is taught in the *Larger Sutra*, the Chinese translation ascribed to Saṃghavarman (Kōsōgai) of the Wu Dynasty (A.D. 252), as the forty-eight Vows of Amida, the most important being the 18th Vow. *Hongan* has been translated as Original Vow, Original Prayer, etc., but Primal Vow is preferred because the dual implications of *pūrva* seem to be suggested by the word 'primal', which is defined in Webster's *Third International Dictionary*: "1. of or relating to the first period or state, original, primitive. 2. first in importance, fundamental, principal." However, the Primal Vow is prior even to the first stage or earliest age, being beyond time, and is even more basic than that which is fundamental. In fact, it is expressive of that which comes even before the first word.

Pure Land (*jōdo* 浄土) A term coined in Chinese Buddhism to bring out the basic meaning of *sukhāvatī* which is directly translated as the realm of ultimate bliss, peaceful bliss, peaceful rest, and so forth. *Sukha*, bliss, is contrasted to *duḥkha*, our world of pain. However, "Pure Land" also has basis in the idea that the realm of enlightened beings has been purified of blind passion and human defilements (*buddhakṣetrapariśuddhi*). T'an-luan said that because nothing is tainted by human ignorance or defilement, it is called the Pure Land. Shinran described it as the land of Immeasurable Light, presided over by the Buddha of Inconceivable Light. The understanding is that it is not a geographical place which radiates gleaming rays of light but that it is a way to express a formless reality through concrete form or imagery. The Pure Land is also called the "fulfilled land," because it was established as the consequence of fulfilling Amida's forty-eight Vows for the salvation of all beings.

Religious practice (*gyō* 行) Unlike religious traditions which stress "faith," Buddhism has considered "religious practice" as necessary for enlightenment. A common formula in Mahayana Buddhism has four stages: pure faith in the validity of a teaching, intellectual understanding of the contents of the teaching, religious practice which incorporates the teaching into one's being, and the ultimate attainment of enlightenment. There are two major types of religious practice: meditative and non-meditative. Meditative practices include all forms of single-minded concentration, whether sitting in the lotus position, walking meditation, chanting of mantras, visualization of mandalas and Buddha images, etc., and non-meditative practices include the observance of precepts, selfless giving, daily worship, and other forms of religious rituals. Shinran rejects all of these as "sundry practices" which cannot lead to real enlightenment. For him the only authentic religious practice is the countless aeons of effort, thought, discipline, and merit accumulated by Dharmākara Bodhisattva, viz. Amida Buddha. Thus, the only true religious practice leading to enlightenment is that of the Buddha, and man partakes of its benefits by saying the nembutsu, which is the practice especially selected by Amida as eminently suitable and efficacious for all people in all ages. Thus saying the nembutsu is called "great practice," meaning that it is not the practice of man but that of the Buddha. When the essence of this great practice is realized in the heart and mind, it is called shinjin.

Same as Maitreya (*miroku ni onaji* 弥勒に同じ) Since the enlightenment of the person of shinjin has already been settled by the working of Amida, his Buddhahood is necessary and inevitable. This is comparable to the status of Maitreya Bodhisattva who now resides in Tushita Heaven awaiting his appearance in this world as a Buddha, succeeding Śākyamuni. Both are just one step before

Buddhahood; in this sense, the person of shinjin is the same as Maitreya.

Saying the nembutsu (*shōmyō* 称名)　Various expressions, such as reciting, pronouncing, or uttering the nembutsu, are in common use. "Saying the nembutsu," however, sounds most natural and ordinary, suited to the religious life of a Shin Buddhist, whereas reciting implies a mechanical and superficial repetition, pronouncing seems too formal, and uttering may suggest that it is nonsensical and meaningless. While there is nothing extraordinary about saying the nembutsu, the realization attached to it, involving one's whole being, evokes an entirely new universe of meaning. The most profound realization of man possible, plumbing the depths of human existence, is actualized in the simple saying of nembutsu.

Selected Primal Vow (*senjaku hongan* 選択本願)　According to the *Larger Sutra*, in establishing his vow Bodhisattva Dharmākara surveyed all the Buddha Lands and chose from among them those qualities he considered best. In essence, his Primal Vow is to create a certain kind of Pure Land, and each of the forty-eight Vows represents the selection of a particular feature of the land, so that taken together they map out the topography of the Pure Land.

It was Hōnen who established *senjaku* as a term for the principle underlying the particular formulation of the Primal Vow. In the third chapter of *Senjaku-shū*, Hōnen states, "The word 'select' (*senjaku*) which occurs in [the *Dai-amida-kyō*] means to take up and to reject," and goes on to demonstrate its applicability to the individual Vows. The importance of *senjaku* for sentient beings lies in his interpretation of the Eighteenth Vow; that is, the rejection of all other practices and the taking up of the saying of the nembutsu as the single cause for birth in Amida's Land. Since this is the crucial point in Hōnen's teaching, *senjaku hongan* has come to indicate the Eighteenth Vow only, in which the nembutsu as the selected practice is given.

Self-power (*jiriki* 自力)   Term used in contrast to Other Power, the power of Amida's Primal Vow.   Hōnen taught that the practice of recitative nembutsu leads to birth in the Pure Land because it accords with the intent of the Primal Vow, and he rejected all other practices as mixed, secondary, or ineffectual, being based upon finite self-power.   Self-power practice is trying to attain enlightenment by accumulating merits through one's own efforts, such as found in the Nineteenth Vow which reads: "awakening the mind of enlightenment and practicing good deeds of merit, sincerely cherishing the desire to be born in the Pure Land."   Shinran inherited Hōnen's stand against self-power, and defined it as "seeking to attain birth by invoking the names of Buddhas other than Amida and performing good acts other than nembutsu, according to one's particular circumstances and opportunities; and by making oneself worthy through amending the confusion in one's acts, words, and thoughts, confident of one's own powers and guided by one's own calculation" (*Letters of Shinran*, Letter 2).   While self-power generally refers to acts other than the nembutsu, Shinran includes it among self-power acts, if it is done with calculative intentions of attaining birth in the Pure Land, based upon the Twentieth Vow. The various practices, including recitative nembutsu of self-power, contained in the Nineteenth and Twentieth Vows are provisional means that lead ultimately to the Other Power nembutsu of the Eighteenth Vow.   Shinran stressed the mind or attitude brought to recitative nembutsu, rather than the actual saying itself, in defining self-power nembutsu.   Without the complete entrusting to Other Power, the person of self-power or calculative mind invites only endless turmoil in trying to follow the Pure Land path.   Examples of self-power practices include the meditative and non-meditative practices of the *Meditation Sutra* (*jōsan no zen*), mixed practices (*zōgyō zasshu*), sundry goods (*zōzen*), and others.

Seventeenth Vow   One of the most important of the Forty-eight Vows of Amida which states: "If, when I attain Buddhahood, the countless Buddhas throughout the worlds in ten quarters do not all say my Name in praise, may I not attain the supreme enlightenment." Here we see the universal testimony of countless enlightened beings in past, present, and future who attest to the efficacy of the Name embodying the Primal Vow. The Name, containing all the working of Tathagata on behalf of sentient beings, is the central religious symbol of Shin Buddhism, therefore, it is called great practice. Since it is the activity of the Buddha and not that of man, it is called "great," indicating a fundamental difference in the quality of the act. And since it leads to enlightenment without fail, it is called "practice." By undertaking the great practice which is the saying of the Name, we are made to participate in the activity of the Tathagata.

Shin Buddhism (*jōdo-shinshū* 浄土真宗) The term *Jōdo-shinshū* was used by Shinran to describe the true essence (*shinshū*) of the Pure Land teaching of his master, Hōnen. Shinran's successors, however came to use it for the name of their school, with Shinran as the founder, thus distinguishing it from other Pure Land schools which also claimed to succeed in Hōnen's teaching. Today, Shin Buddhism claims the largest number of followers of any school of Japanese Buddhism.

Shinjin (*shinjin* 信心) The realization of Other Power in which human calculation is negated through the working of Amida Buddha. It denotes the central religious experience of Shin Buddhism, and literally means man's "true, real and sincere heart and mind" (*makoto no kokoro*), which is given by Amida Buddha. This heart-mind has basically two aspects: a non-dichotomous identity wherein the heart and mind of Amida and the heart and mind of man are one, and a dichotomous relationship wherein the two are mutually exclusive and in dynamic interaction. Used as an adjective, *shin* 信 (which is different from the term Shin 真 Buddhism) has the meaning of "true, real and sincere." As a verb, it means "to entrust oneself to the Buddha," an act which is made possible by the working of the true, real and sincere heart and mind of Amida Buddha. These two meanings are always inseparable. Thus, while shinjin is an experience on the part of man, its source, its contents, and its consummation are to be found not in man but in Buddha.

Shinjin has commonly been translated as "faith," but we have felt that that term, so strongly and variously colored by its usage in the Judeo-Christian tradition, would only blur the precision of the meaning of the original. Paul Tillich has stated:

There is hardly a word in the religious language, both theological and popular, which is subject to more misunderstandings, distortions and questionable definitions than the word "faith." It belongs to those terms which need healing before they can be used for the healing of men. Today the term "faith" is more productive of disease than of health. It confuses, misleads, creates alternately skepticism and fanaticism, intellectual resistance and emotional surrender, rejection of genuine religion and subjection to substitutes. Indeed, one is tempted to suggest that the word "faith" should be dropped completely; but desirable as that may be it is hardly possible. A powerful tradition [Christianity] protects it. "Introductory Remarks," *Dynamics of Faith* (New York: Harper & Row, 1957), ix.

Supreme nirvana (*mujō-nehan* 無上涅槃) Nirvana is the goal of the Buddhist life, where the false self is annihilated, never to emerge again, and a new being of true compassion and true wisdom, concerned with the welfare of all beings, is born. Supreme nirvana is contrasted to nirvana limited to personal emancipation.

Surpassing conceptual understanding (*fukashigi* 不可思議) "Inconceivable" has been the common translation for *fukashigi*, and is accurate if properly understood. *Fukashigi* means that something cannot be understood by conventional means; nevertheless, it is within the awareness of man. The awareness, however, cannot exhaust its depth, which is fathomless. Thus, *fukashigi* means that while something can be known, it is not subject to intellectual analysis. This is the reason for the admonition against trying to reason out the meaning of "no selfworking is true working." "Mystery" might be an apt translation for this term, but it is confused with mysteriousness and mystification in popular understanding, so it should be used with care.

Tathagata (*nyorai* 如来) A synonym of Buddha, frequently used by Shinran to refer to Amida Buddha. The term is derived from combining *tathā-āgata* which means to come from suchness, or from joining *tathā-gata* which means to go to suchness. In East Asian Buddhism the term Tathagata is preferred over the term Buddha because of its dynamic, religious connotation; and the idea that Tathagata "comes from suchness" is favored over the other form of "going to suchness."

Tathagata of unhindered light filling the ten quarters (*jinjippō-mugekō-nyorai* 尽十方無碍光如来) A synonym for Amida Buddha, sometimes shortened to Unhindered Light. According to Shinran, light is the "form" or manifestation of transcendental wisdom, and since nothing can obstruct or hinder its penetrating illumination, it is called unhindered. This unhindered light fills the entire universe, the ten quarters referring to the eight points of the compass, the nadir and the zenith. The function of unhindered light working on man has various stages: it illuminates and penetrates the hardest substance in the world—the blind, stubborn clinging to the false ego, forged through countless aeons of time; it melts this hardest substance in the world, transforming it into a supple and resilient being both in mind and body; and it nurtures a new being, a person of shinjin whose necessary and inevitable attainment is Buddhahood.

Ten transgressions (*jū-aku* 十悪) The Buddhist precepts against 1) destroying life, 2) theft, 3) adultery, 4) lying, 5) harsh words, 6) speaking ill of others, 7) idle talk, 8) greed, 9) anger, 10) wrong views.

Threefold Shinjin (*sanshin* 三信) The threefold shinjin contained in the eighteenth Vow are (1) sincere mind, (2) trust and (3) aspiration for birth in the Pure Land, each of which, according to Shinran, is completely free of doubt, including self-will, calculation, and self-power. Hōnen identified them with the three minds of the *Meditation Sutra* as necessary mental attitudes of the nembutsu practicer. Shinran, however, regarded them as the manifestations of the working of Other Power, stating that the sincere mind of the Buddha enters the ignorant and deluded mind of man, causing in him the experience of joyful faith and prompting him to aspire for the Pure Land. He also summarized the threefold shinjin into One-mind which is none other than Other Power. Thus, the threefold shinjin can be seen as the true and real mind of the Buddha working, or as its manifestation in the heart and mind of the person of shinjin.

Three minds (*sanshin* 三心) The three minds appear in the *Meditation Sutra* and include (1) sincere mind, (2) deep mind, and (3) desire for birth by accumulating merit. According to Shan-tao, the three are necessary mental attitudes of the Pure Land practicer who seeks to be born in the Pure Land. Such a person, thus, must manifest a sincere mind, a profound realization of his own karmic evil, as well as Amida's boundless compassion, and a willingness to share with others the fruits of the religious life. In Shinran's understanding such an interpretation of three minds is a self-power approach and should be distinguished from the threefold shinjin of the *Larger Sutra of Immeasurable Life*. However, he also stated that the covert meaning of the three minds is identical with the threefold shinjin, both revealing the working of Other Power. This conflicting interpretation is resolved by Shinran's theory of "explicit and implicit hermeneutics."

True compassion; Great compassion (*daihi* 大悲) The English equivalent for *daihi* is *mahā-karuṇā* in Sanskrit, and it constitutes the essence of the Buddha of Immeasurable Life and Light. According to Webster's *International Dictionary*, compassion means to bear with or suffer with another being: it is a "deep feeling for and understanding of misery or suffering and the

concomitant desire to promote its alleviation; spiritual consciousness of the personal tragedy of another or others and selfless
tenderness directed toward it." While this definition seems to
convey the idea of Buddhist compassion, it is inadequate because of
the distinction between self and other, for in Buddhism compassion
goes beyond any division or dichotomy between self and other into
the world of complete identity. The basic meaning of "sorrow"
in *daihi* or "lament" in *mahā-karuṇā* attempts to show this selfsame
identity wherein the misery, suffering, or personal tragedy of another
is none other than one's very own. Such a non-dichotomous
compassion is guided by *prajñā*, a wisdom which surpasses conventional thinking and feeling and moves in non-dichotomous
perception (*nirvikalpajñāna*).

Truly settled ones (*shōjōju* 正定聚) A term descriptive of those
who will attain enlightenment without fail. Alternate translations
used in the past include such terms as the truly assured ones, truly
determined ones, etc., but truly settled ones is preferred because
"assured" lacks the definitiveness of the original expression and
"determined" sounds willful, forced and unnatural, whereas
"settled" connotes the wholeness, naturalness and peacefulness of
one whose perfect enlightenment has been decided and is only a
matter of time. This word was originally used to describe the
bodhisattva who had reached a stage where enlightenment would be
attained without question. In the Pure Land tradition prior to
Shinran it referred to those beings born in the Pure Land who
without fail will attain enlightenment because of the ideal environment conducive to religious life. For Shinran, however, the truly
settled ones are the people of shinjin in this life who have been
awakened by the Primal Vow here and now. They are also described as being in the stage of non-retrogression.

Turn-about (*eshin* 廻心) The radical conversion experience brought
about by the working of Other Power, whereby the center of one's
being, the mind of self-power, is overturned and abandoned. Man,

thus, gives himself up completely to the working of Amida's Primal Vow.

Virtue, Merit (*kudoku* 功徳)　The original Japanese, *kudoku*, is translated into two English terms, virtue and merit, in order to differentiate its dual meaning.　"Virtue" is used in the Aristotelian sense of inherent power realizing itself fully, but having the added quality of bringing with it immeasurable virtue of benefits to oneself and others, being the undefiled wisdom and compassion of the Buddha.　The Name, embodying this wisdom and compassion, is virtue incarnate given to man; thus, when he says the Name, he also realizes the the virtue of the Buddha.　When *kudoku* is translated as "merit," it refers to something man-made and therefore requires frequent attention to this matter in regards to the nembutsu.　Self-power practice requires the constant repetition of nembutsu in order to accumulate merit for birth in the Pure Land.

LIST OF
NAMES AND TITLES

Brahma-net Sutra (梵網經, j. *Bommō kyō*) A sutra whose exposition of precepts—particularly of the Mahayana precepts to be observed by all Buddhists, without distinction of priest and lay—has been of great importance in East Asian Buddhism.

Collection of Passages on the Nembutsu of the Selected Primal Vow (選択本願念佛集, *Senjaku Hongan Nembutsu-shū*) The work by Hōnen which, expounding the nembutsu that is based on Other Power, marks the founding of the Pure Land school in Japan.

Fa-chao (法照, j. Hosshō) T'ang dynasty Pure Land monk and second generation disciple of Tz'u-min. He is remembered for his arrangement of nembutsu chant in fivefold harmony. Because of his success in spreading the Pure Land teaching he was known as 'the second Shan-tao.'

Hōnen (法然, 1133–1212) Founder of the independent Pure Land school and teacher of Shinran, who considered him to be the seventh patriarch of Shin Buddhism. Also known as Genkū.

Hymns of Birth in the Pure Land (往生禮讚, j. *Ōjōraisan*) A collection of hymns by Shan-tao arranged to be chanted at the six times of the day: sunset, evening, night, late night, sunrise, and midday.

Jikaku (慈覚, 794–864) High-ranking Japanese monk of the Tendai school who studied in China and transmitted esoteric Tendai teachings to Japan. Also known as Ennin 圓仁.

Larger Sutra of Immeasurable Life (*Sukhāvatī-vyūha sūtra*, 大無量壽經, j. *Daimuryōju kyō*) The scripture which relates the origin and fulfillment of the Primal Vow. It was translated a number of times into Chinese, and of the five extant versions, Shinran relied chiefly on that of Samghavarman (康僧鎧, j. Kōsōgai) dated 252 A.D.

Meditation Sutra (観無量壽經, j. *Kanmuryōju kyō*) More fully, "the Sutra of Meditation on Amida Buddha," it describes meditative practices centering on Amida and his land, various types of meritorious works, and concludes with a prescription of vocal nembutsu. It survives only in a Chinese translation made in 424 A.D.

Hymns of the Nembutsu Liturgy (法事讃, j. *Hōjisan*) A complete liturgy of hymns arranged by Shan-tao.

Hymns of the Nembutsu Liturgy in Fivefold Harmony (五會法事讃, j. *Goehōjisan*) A complete liturgy of hymns arranged by Fa-chao, with musical elements based on the descriptions of the sounds in the Pure Land found in the *Larger Sutra*.

Shan-tao (善導, j. Zendō 613–681) An important Jōdo master in Chinese Buddhism; the 5th patriarch of Shin Buddhism.

Commentary on the Meditation Sutra (観經疏, j. *Kangyō sho*) Shan-tao's exhaustive four-part exposition of the *Meditation Sutra*.

List of Names and Titles

Smaller Sutra of Immeasurable Life (*Sukhāvatī-vyūha sūtra*, 阿彌 陀經, j. *Amida kyō*) One of the three central scriptures of Jōdo Buddhism. In it Śākyamuni preaches the splendors of the Buddha Land and the necessity of aspiration to be born there. Translated into Chinese by Kumārajīva in 402 A.D.

T'an-luan (曇鸞, j. Donran 476–542) The first significant figure of Jōdo Buddhism in China; the third patriarch of Shin Buddhism.

Treatise on the Pure Land (浄土論, j. *Jōdoron*) A work attributed to Vasubandhu based in great part on the *Larger Sutra of Immeasurable Life* and dealing with the aspiration and practice for birth in the Pure Land. It survives only in the Chinese translation of Bodhiruci (菩提流支).

Tz'u-min (慈愍, j. Jimin) T'ang dynasty Chinese monk and the next major Pure Land master after Shan-tao. Studied in India for twelve years and propagated the nembutsu among the common people upon his return to China.

Vasubandhu (世親 or 天親, j. Seshin or Tenjin ca. 320–400) Great Indian Buddhist thinker; the second Shin patriarch after Nāgārjuna.

NOTE ON THE TEXT

Shinran is known to have copied his *Notes on 'Essentials of Faith Alone'* (唯信鈔文意, *Yuishinshō-mon'i*) a number of times during his last years, and manuscripts bearing dates ranging from 1250 to 1257 have come down to us. We have taken as our basic text the one dated the 19th of the eight month, Shōka 1 (1257), in the Hōyōbon edition, included in *Shinshū Shōgyō Zensho* (Kyoto, 1941), volume 2, 621–638. An edition of this text can also be found in the *Taishō Shinshū Daizōkyō*, volume 83, no. 2658, 705–710.

This Shōka text is no longer extant in Shinran's own hand, but it has been historically the most widespread version, as evidenced by the fact that it survives in the greatest number of old manuscript copies; it was also employed by the traditional commentators.

In recent times two nearly identical autograph manuscripts have come to light, dated within several weeks of each other, both in the first month of Kōgen 2 (also 1257), about seven months before the Shōka text. This Kōgen text can be found in *Shinshū Shōgyō Zensho*, volume 2, 639–655, and in the *Taishō Shinshū Daizōkyō*, volume 83, 699–704. Although the differences between the Kōgen and Shōka texts are quite minor on the whole, we have chosen to follow the Shōka text because in a number of passages it gives slightly expanded, and therefore more easily understandable, explanations. We have, however, referred to the Kōgen text throughout, and in the few instances in which the two texts seem to differ in meaning or implication, we have adopted the autograph version. These are indicated by footnotes. In addition, where there are significant differences in expression, we have translated the autograph version in footnotes.

The oldest and most reliable text of Seikaku's *Essentials of Faith Alone* (唯信鈔, *Yuishinshō*) is that of Shinran's copy dated Kanki 2 (1230), and we have followed it in our translation here. It can be found in *Shinshū Shōgyō Zensho*, volume 2, 739–756, and in the *Daizōkyō*, volume 83, no. 2675, 910–915.

Abridgments

As Shinran says in the postscript to *Notes on 'Essentials of Faith Alone'*, his intent was to explain the meaning of passages in Chinese to people unable to read Chinese characters; he therefore found it necessary at points simply to give direct translations of individual words; that is, to identify characters by giving their Japanese readings. Since we have elected to translate the Chinese quotations as well as Shinran's explanations, the necessity for such commentary has completely disappeared in several passages, where a literal rendering of the text would result in tautologies such as "**Vow** means vow" or "**Gold** means gold." As the postscript indicates, Shinran himself was well aware of the redundancy in his explanations for the educated reader. We have felt, however, that to include such passages would only distract the reader and ultimately misrepresent the text. For this reason we have abridged the following passages from the translation:

Page 36, line 22, after "Bodhisattva Dharmākara."
   Made the Universal Vow: to make means "to establish," "to accomplish." **Universal** means "wide," "to spread." **Vow** means "vow."
Page 40, last line, after "This is a metaphor."
   Can means "able." **Make** means "to cause to do." **Bits of rubble** is literally "tile" and "pebbles." **Change into gold: change** into means "turn into"; **gold** is "gold."

Page 46, line 22, after "difficult to accept."

The meaning of this passage from the *Larger Sutra* is that to hear this sutra and realize shinjin is the most difficult among all difficulties. There is nothing that is more difficult.

Page 47, line 22, after "threefold mind."

Necessarily attains birth: **necessarily** means "without fail." **Attain** means "to attain": "to attain" here means to attain birth.

Bibliography

The following commentaries were consulted in making the translation of *Notes on 'Essentials of Faith Alone'*:

Hokkai (1768–1834), *Yuishinshō-mon'i shimmi roku*, in *Shinshū taikei*, vol. 22 (Tokyo: Kokusho kankōkai, 1917).

Jinrei (1749–1817), *Yuishinshō-mon'i roku*, in *Shinshū zensho*, vol. 42 (Tokyo: Kokusho kankōkai, 1913).

Kiritani Junnin, "Yuishinshō-mon'i," in *Shinshū seiten kōsan zenshū*, vol. 5 (Tokyo: Kokusho kankōkai, 1934).

Rizen (1754–1819), *Yuishinshō-mon'i gigai*, in *Shinshū zensho*, vol. 47.

Umehara Shinryū, *Yuishinshō-mon'i kōgi* (Kyoto: Kenshin gakuen, 1937).

INDEX TO THE TRANSLATIONS

THE SHIN BUDDHISM TRANSLATION SERIES

The Shin Buddhism Translation Series initiated in 1978 is a twelve year program designed to present the principle Shin Buddhist scriptures in scholarly and yet lucid English translation. We have begun with a plan to publish all of Shinran's writings, starting with the works in Japanese of his later years and including a complete version of his monumental work in classical Chinese, *Kyōgyōshinshō*. The entire project is undertaken as one of the activities commemorating the accession to the office of Monshu, or head of the Hompa Hongwanji temple, by Koshin Ohtani in 1977, and through it the Hongwanji hopes to make the scriptures of Shin Buddhism widely available to readers outside of Japan.

A translation of a religious text requires meticulous attention to detail if it is to be truly meaningful. The present volume, *Notes on 'Essentials of Faith Alone'*, has benefitted from a careful review by an advisory board that included:

Ryosetsu Fujiwara	Keiwa Ishida	Mitsuyuki Ishida
Kenryo Kumata	Hakunin Matsuo	Gadjin Nagao
Ryusei Takeda	Shoho Takemura	Yoshifumi Ueda
Ryushin Uryuzu		

The advisory board has generously provided guidance in the interpretation of the original text and its accurate rendering into English; final responsibility for any errors that may remain, however, must be placed with the editorial and translation staff.

Translation work, by the very knowledge of the original text that it demands, severely limits the degree of critical review possible by the translators themselves. We have sought to walk the thin line dividing mere literalism from excessive interpretation, hoping to avoid lapses from comprehensible English on the one hand and from faithfulness to the text on the other. Ultimately we must depend on the reader, and we welcome any responses that will aid us in revision in the future.

We would also like to acknowledge the invaluable suggestions and comments on this particular project solicited and received from many persons in America and Europe active in the propagation and teaching of Shin Buddhism.

Koyo Okuda, Supervisor
Hongwanji International Department